Developing Spiritually Sensitive Children

Developing Spiritually Sensitive Children

Olive J. Alexander

Bethany Fellowship INC.
MINNEAPOLIS, MINNESOTA 55438

Scripture references are taken from the Revised Standard Version
of the Bible, copyrighted 1946, © 1952, © 1971, © 1973.

Published by Bethany Fellowship, Inc.
6820 Auto Club Road, Minneapolis, Minnesota 55438

Printed in the United States of America

Library of Congress Cataloging in Publication Data

Alexander, Olive J 1939-
    Developing spiritually sensitive children.

    1. Children—Religious life. 2. Parent and child. I. Title.
BV4571.2.A4   649'.7   80-23603
ISBN 0-87123-111-5

About the Author

Olive J. Alexander is a housewife in Hereford, Texas, and the mother of two teenage children. She attended Baylor University and Brown University and received her B.A. from the latter. She has been a staff member with Youth With A Mission in Hawaii, a Montessori method teacher, a copy editor, and recently has been teaching high school math. She has also written a play, published verse, magazine articles, and an oratorio.

Foreword

It delights the heart of God and good people everywhere to observe a family living in the warm glow of love resulting from Christian principles given us through the Master's manual. Children not only grow but also blossom in such a sunlit environment.

I happily watched this process in the Alexander family for over three years as both Eric and Paula gently entered their early teens. I was impressed by the process and for this reason am delighted that the principles have been made public through this book.

Unfortunately, not all children have a loving Christian home. Many know only half a home. Some know none at all. Instead of a home, millions of miserable little ones, whom Jesus wants to come to Him, know only a "battleground." Jesus said it would be better to be weighted and dropped to the bottom of the ocean than to burden and suffocate these children with offenses. Yet through ignorance, insensitivity, bitterness and strife, sins are multiplied to the "fourth generation." We must break the chain through the Spirit of Truth.

If adults are not to "walk in the counsel of the ungodly, nor stand in the way of sinners, nor sit in the seat of the scornful," then surely God wants something even better for children. No wonder He included so much help for parents, enabling them to "train up a child in the way he should go."

This book has Bible basis and Christian content with practical, common-sense application. The insights included will delight you as you read and study them. And you in turn will delight God and others as you apply them in your family.

Let the author lead you into the "garden of the little ones" and page by page see the world from a child's eyes. You can train children properly "in the way they should go" only when *you* obey Jesus—becoming like a child, leaving the complex insensitive world of most adults and entering the sensitive, uncomplicated world of children, for this is "the kingdom of heaven."

Loren Cunningham
International Director, Youth With A Mission
Kailua-Kona, Hawaii, Sept. 1980

Preface

This is a book about serving our littlest brethren—children. Jesus said, "If you do it unto one of the least of them, you have done it unto me." Service to children is service to Jesus.

The purpose of this book is to encourage parents and other adults in this service, helping them to understand what service actually is and suggesting ways in which they can implement into their daily situations and relationships what God says about children. When we understand not only the process of a child's physical and spiritual development but also come to believe and see that the Holy Spirit himself is participating in that process, we can more easily free our children to minister to God, to each other, and to the adults in their lives.

I cannot think of a more neglected subject in the whole area of child-adult relations than the one I propose. It is neglected because most adults have a wrong view of children. Children are often thought of as small persons who need to be told many things, who need to be corrected continually and kept on the "straight and narrow," who need to be restricted and disciplined and taught to obey. This is certainly true. But we need to be reminded that these are our own needs as well. In fact, if you trace the word "discipline" in this book, you will find that each time it appears it refers to adult self-discipline and not to the spanking of children or the hows, whys, and whens of that procedure.

I spank children when I need to spank them. But I do

not talk about that here. Others have given ample instruction on that type of correction. But no one seems to be dealing with the need for adult self-discipline in regard to children. Therefore, I talk much about that subject.

I am convinced that we can eliminate many of the problems we have with children and many of the griefs and problems they have with us if we humbly consider the role discipline should play in our own lives.

We adults need to be disciplined persons. We need to learn to obey God instantly, cheerfully, and completely. We need to complete the things we begin. So many of the character defects we see in children are much more evident in our own lives. Because of this, much of a child's growth in the Lord depends upon whether or not we are willing to change—willing to build new habits, new ways of responding.

We must begin to treat children in the way we would want to be treated if we were their size and strength. Jesus pointed this out in Matthew 7:12, "Whatever you would that men should do to you, do ye even so to them." Applying this commandment to our relationship with small persons who only have two, four, six, or eight years of experience in living and who are not yet "all together" in muscle coordination, reasoning ability, and sufficient experience and knowledge necessary for good judgments will take concentrated effort, determination and a good deal of imagination.

It will also touch every area of our lives: the living space we share with them and how we arrange it for their comfort, growth, and development; the tone of voice we use when we communicate with them; the vocabulary we use; the things we place into their environments and the things we keep out; the way we use our time in regard to them and their needs; and how we pray for and with them.

The principles involved are God's, but the expression of these truths will be as varied as the individuals concerned.

If you are committed to finding the Lord's ways in each circumstance and for each child, He will bless your relationship and ministry.

Nations have been blessed or cursed by mothers and fathers. Hitler was once a child and so was John Wesley. The difference was made by a mother who followed the guidance of the Holy Spirit in rearing her sons. For Susanna Wesley there was no higher, more important job for her than to raise her children to know the Lord.

Christian parents can rejoice in taking their responsibilities. What we do has eternal results. Our faithful service to our children will also affect our own lives, and the society and country in which we live.

God will help us. God will guide us. He wants to speak counsel in our ears if we are willing to listen to Him. Even now He is actively loving, helping, teaching, leading, guiding, calling forth, equipping, instructing, and growing the small persons we have produced. It remains for us to get *lined up* with what He is doing in them and through them. So let's take another look at our children. Let's look at them the way God does.

And let's listen to Him. He will speak to our hearts. He will speak through His Word. And He will speak to us through the children themselves. That is His kindness to us: we are *surrounded* by His loving counsel, and we have no need to distrust our ability to hear and to obey Him who calls us to serve the little children in our world.

Contents

1. Let the Children Come

I was sitting on the edge of the low stage, singing a spiritual with all my heart, "I Want Jesus to Walk with Me." The young people gathered in the basement of this downtown church were up front for the "action," but toward the back a few grown-ups, along with their toddlers, had joined our group.

Suddenly, one small child about eighteen months old crawled down from his mother's lap, trotted up the aisle, climbed up on my lap, and leaned back against my right arm, gazing intently into my face while I sang the soft, slow song with its deeply moving words. For a few short minutes each person in the room was wrapped up in a unique "oneness."

Then, after a few seconds of silence, the mood changed. The little child gave a start, looked at me in a different way and began to cry for his mother. Quickly I slipped him down from my knees, and he ran back to the security of his mother's arms.

What had happened? Why had he left his mother and climbed up on me?

Many times before I had heard mothers of our Christian community tell how their little ones relaxed and smiled as they responded to the name of Jesus on the lips of their parents. And I had believed them. After all, Jesus himself said, "Let the children come to me, and do not hinder them; for to such belongs the kingdom of heaven" (Matt. 19:14).

I realized that I had seen a present-day demonstration of this principle. The child who had climbed onto my lap as

14

I sang was responding to Jesus. By means of a song, the Holy Spirit had spoken directly to this little child, and he had responded to the presence of Jesus—a response which came from his heart, bypassing his understanding. There were no barriers between this child and Jesus. However, when the song was finished, he immediately sensed the difference and acted as he would have with any stranger.

In a new way, this incident opened up my understanding of children and the development of their relationship with God. I realized that as an adult I was a key ingredient: the tone of my voice, the choice of words I used, the way I touched them, the things I put into their world (in this instance, a song)—all these influence the eternal destiny of children with whom I come in contact. I saw that I could touch children in the place of Jesus. And so can you. We can and must bring children to Jesus.

At no other time in history have adults felt such a terrific strain in raising their own children. Instead of being a source of joy and contentment, children are often considered to be a source of humiliation, anxiety, and fear. Many parents are confessing that they do not understand their children, they cannot "handle" their children, and they cannot give their children what they really need. Parents have lost self-esteem and confidence, two very necessary ingredients for the task of parenting.

How then can we establish a relationship with our children so that we do not feel guilty and condemned all the time? What can we do to counteract and avoid our failures and sins against them?

We can know a child's height and weight as well as something of his intellectual ability and social awareness; but unless we also know what God is saying to the child and to us about the child, we will remain in the dark. Fortunately, however, wisdom is ours for the asking: "If any of you lacks wisdom, let him ask God. . . . " I have asked, and the answer is unbelievably simple: *all of us, of all ages, are to be living under the lordship of Jesus Christ.*

The wisdom God gave me began to grow as I looked at everything in the light of His Kingdom. When children are considered, first and foremost, as brothers and sisters in Christ, instead of mere children to be seen and not heard, our lives will be turned upside down and inside out. Instead of being ones who are "always under foot," our children will be recognized as those who are made in the image of God. Their wonderful capacities to communicate, to know, to reason, to perceive, to feel, to enjoy, to make things, and to have relationships will be developed in ways we have never imagined. The children will not only benefit but we will experience the satisfaction God intended we should have as families under God's rule. Not only will He be able to love and speak through us to the children, but the children also will be released to minister to us.

The Holy Spirit demonstrated this truth to me when my own children were still very young. Another woman and I were sitting together at the kitchen table, doing some serious talking. The children, then six and four, were playing in the backyard (a good place for them to be when there is an adult in the house who has serious problems and a vocabulary which youngsters do not need to hear).

They had greeted her when she first came to the house, but then left her alone. She was not a person whom the children especially liked. I mention this so that you will feel the import of what I want to describe to you. There were other adults who were very special to Eric and Paula, but she was not. She reeked of stale tobacco smoke and talked with a very loud voice.

When our talk was finished, the woman and I agreed to pray once again about her situation. Before we started, however, the children joined us. Evidently they had heard us through the screen door and knew that we were ready to pray together. So they came into the kitchen quietly and each put his hands on the older lady's shoulders. Each prayed out a few simple thoughts such as "Take away all her fears," and "Give her faith to trust in you," and "Let her know you love her." Then there was silence. They had done all the praying that needed to be done. Quietly, they went away, back to the backyard with its sandbox and climber.

We adults sat still, lost in the peace of God's response to their prayers. They had said everything for us. There was nothing else to say. I do not know how they "knew" to come in. They had not been asked. But obviously they had been in touch with God.

We too need to be in touch with God so that we do not prevent the normal development of each child's relationship with God. We need to observe and watch children. Each one is unique. We need to learn how to listen, both to them and to God's quiet voice speaking through them.

Sometimes we see, but we do not really perceive. Sometimes we hear, but we do not hear what our children are really trying to say. We hear the jumble of childish babbling but do not discern God's activity in and through them. Unless we increase our expectation in relation to our children, we will miss most of their potential as "expressors" of God.

Let me tell you about one time when I almost missed what God was doing. My husband was a thousand miles away from us one night and called long distance about an impending crisis. The situation seemed critical to me, so after I hung up the telephone I called Eric and Paula, then eight and six.

"Daddy really needs you to pray for him," I said. "He needs your prayers right now." I was sick in bed with the flu myself and knew that I could not get to our Friday night prayer meeting that evening, so I figured that the children and I would pray right then.

All they did, however, was to look at each other and go downstairs. I drifted off to sleep with a sigh, thinking, "Oh, well, they didn't pay any attention to Earl's prayer request. But they're only kids . . . "

A while later I was awakened by their pulling me and shaking me. It was dusk and we always walked to our friends' home for the prayer meeting before dusk.

"Mama, we're going to the prayer meeting by taxi. But you need to give us a quarter to make the money come out enough."

"Why on earth are you going to the prayer meeting? By taxi? And how . . . ?" Finally fully awake, my dismay became apparent. But they seemed astonished at my questions.

"You said Daddy needed us to pray for him. Marcella [their teenage friend who lived downstairs] called a taxi for us, and we got out all our money. But we need you to loan us a quarter to have enough."

Speechless, I fished out a quarter from my purse. What could I say to them? Of course they had to get to the prayer group so the grown-ups could join them in praying for their father.

The following week my friend who hosted the prayer meeting told me what happened. According to her, the two children burst in the door, going directly into the prayer circle. "You need to help us pray for our daddy," they said. Intercession began. After a few minutes the children were satisfied and began to drift in and out of the prayer circle— outside to climb a tree, back to join the singing and to "check on what's going on," then to their friend's bedroom to peer through his microscope at a newly mounted insect, and again back to the prayer circle. It was the children's customary prayer-meeting-night activity. But they had accomplished their big business first: prayer for their father.

I had doubted whether I was "getting through" to the children about this urgent prayer request. But in the end I learned a valuable lesson. I am only a part of the working out of God's plan for my children's lives. The Holy Spirit himself is the chief factor in their lives. Therefore, I do not have to act as if I were totally responsible for their submission to His lordship. Since God created each child and knows him intimately, He will make use of His direct access to him and will actively engage each child in some type of inner communion.

God is so much greater than we think and far more active than we realize in the lives of our children. Several years ago, Jay, a thirteen-year-old friend of our son, Eric, responded in a wonderful way to God's activity within him.

Jay had a habit of listening to God and talking with Him in the early morning hours. Day after day God kept saying, "Give your skateboard to Eric." Finally, one day He spoke very pointedly. "Jay, if you love Me, give Eric your skateboard."

Jay gave Eric his skateboard, not because he knew that Eric longed to have a skateboard but in response to the quiet voice of God. Although the skateboard was his dearest possession, he valued his loving relationship with Jesus far more.

Children who hear God and follow His wishes make wonderful companions. And adults who know how to discern God speaking through a child will reap a double blessing: spiritual companionship with the child and humility before the Lord.

My husband, Earl, and I were sitting together on our green sofa one day when Eric, eight, passed through the room on his way to play in the backyard.

Suddenly he stopped and looked at us rather seriously.

"God says, 'Feed my sheep!' " He paused and then repeated it. " 'Feed my sheep!' " As soon as he had said this he disappeared through the door into the yard.

All Earl and I could do was look at each other in amazement as the full meaning and impact of his words began to relate to our conversation and life-style. We felt that we had heard God speak through a little boy's words. And from that day on our lives began to follow another direction. Those brief words led us into commitment to good nutrition and adequate food for people. It also led us into a further commitment to the spiritual feeding of those who have never experienced the joy and peace which comes from knowing God personally through His Son, Jesus. Once we began to pursue this direction, we discovered that the Holy Spirit had been showing people everywhere what God's concerns are—good food for their bodies, good food for their minds and souls, and good food for their spirits.

And God showed us the importance of children also. They are future leaders. Watching them, observing them, and listening to what the Spirit is saying to them and through them helps us discern the next areas to be entered into in God's Kingdom. God used Eric to open new doors for us to present the message that God's people could live well and relate well with their children, receiving good things from God through them.

Sometimes I wonder what would have happened had we not accepted this word from a little child. No doubt we would have missed much excitement along with the satisfaction of knowing that we are fulfilling God's plan for us as individuals and as a family.

Besides this, however, had we not been sensitive to the activity of the Holy Spirit in Eric, we could have unknowingly built a barrier between Eric and any future promptings of the Holy Spirit. Instead of being free to express his understanding of God, he would have feared rejection, eventually stifling the beautifully simple responses of a heart which is open to God.

This childlike openness is something we must cherish and guard for our children lest they become strangers to us. God desires that we maintain this openness toward the Holy Spirit and also toward each other, for without it He finds it difficult to speak to us and to bring us into the full unity of His Spirit.

This was vividly demonstrated to us when the Lord brought our family into YWAM ("Youth With A Mission") in Hawaii. Eleven of us were sitting in a circle discussing our preparations for going to Kauai, one of the neighboring islands. We were going on "evangelistic outreach" and Paula, eleven, and Eric, thirteen, were part of the team.

After a while we decided to ask God if He had anything on His mind that we needed to know. We waited silently, going around the circle so each person could have a chance to share anything he heard or understood with the rest of us.

"Glue" was a word that was impressed upon Paula's heart during the silence. But it took courage and a willingness to be open with the rest of us for Paula to speak it out. She could not understand why the word "glue" would come to her at such a time. How could it be appropriate?

Finally, looking rather sheepish, she broke the silence. "Glue," said Paula.

"Glue!" Eric exclaimed. "That's what I heard!" He and she had both heard the same word while praying.

The friend sitting next to Eric quickly spoke up. "Listen to the scripture verse I have to share. 'In Him all things hold together' (Col. 1:17)."

We understood then. We were together as a team because of Him. He was the "glue" that bound us together, the "glue" that strengthened us and kept us from falling apart under pressure from the enemy.

Again the openness and simplicity of a child's response to God's truth ministered to all of us. Obviously, God is not a respecter of persons. In the same way that the Holy Spirit works through adults, He also desires to work through children. And it is up to us, the older brothers and sisters in Christ, to uncover, encourage, and cooperate with the power of the Holy Spirit ministering in and through children.

Let me give you three examples of the different ways in

which children fulfill God's purposes for their lives.

First of all, they have a ministry to God. When Eric was five years old, he would spend much of his playtime at school under the big tree, all alone, singing to God and laughing. He was a sociable little person—not at all a recluse. But to be alone with God and to sing to Him and to laugh out of the happiness that would well up in his heart through the singing was far more attractive to him than the regular play with the other children. " . . . have you never read, 'Out of the mouth of babes and sucklings thou hast brought perfect praise'?" (Matt. 21:16).

Children also have a ministry to each other. Two-year-old Sarah had a special way of soothing the franticly crying ones in our nursery at church. The way she carefully looked at them, touching them with her gentle, soft hand made the edgy ones more comfortable. Her little gestures and her intent interest in the other little ones was a ministry that the Holy Spirit worked through her for the comfort and the happiness of all of us in the nursery.

And finally, children have a ministry to those of us who are older than they are.

I was so tired of the wrangling and the shouting among members of a family with whom we were staying. Eric and Paula looked at me and began to analyze what they were observing.

"What Mama needs is a walk to hear the birds," one said to the other. One stood on my right, one on my left. I leaned on their shoulders, my every nerve strung out and dangling, as they steered me out the front door and down the street to the park with its huge cage of birds. Firmly yet gently they led me to the park bench and told me to sit down. "You'll feel better soon. We're gonna go swing."

Minutes grew into half an hour, and at last I heard the birds. The jangling in my body had subsided, and I sighed as I began to enjoy the outdoors.

The children observed me continually from their swings

nearby. Finally they came back to the bench.

"You feel okay now? Ready to go back to the house?"

Yes, I was ready, because I had reaped the benefits of allowing my children to follow the suggestions of God's Spirit within them. Once again I understood the message of Psalm 127:3, "Lo, sons are a heritage from the Lord, the fruit of the womb a reward."

Each of our children, yours and mine, are specially designed gifts given to us by our heavenly Father. And He is asking us to respect, appreciate, and accept them as He does, freeing them to become all that He has created them to be through Jesus, His Son.

"Let the children come to me, and do not hinder them; for to such belongs the kingdom of heaven" (Mark 10:14).

2. Sensitivity Begins with You

The decade of the seventies has been rightly called by some the "ME" generation. Everyone was encouraged to find themselves, to do their own thing, to get involved in the "identity crisis." And many adults did just that. I'm not sure whether they found what they were looking for, but I am convinced that one of the side effects of their adult pursuits has been the neglect of innocent children. Children have been ignored in varying degrees emotionally, spiritually and physically, so that now we have a growing national problem—child abuse.

Perhaps in the eighties we will see a return to the more noble values of family closeness, sharing, and love. Even now the secularists are beginning to recognize the need for responsible adult parenting and have sought to introduce legislation along these lines.

Sensitivity, compassion and the desire to serve cannot be legislated, however. These are results of living under the lordship of Jesus Christ. God is once again encouraging us to make great efforts to restore fellowship and repair broken relationships with the children who live among us. But in order to do this *we* must be prepared to change.

By change I am not speaking of merely acting differently. I am referring to an inner restoration which frees us to be all that a child needs as a parent. For example, a child needs parents who consistently respect him. But how can parents show respect toward their children when they don't respect themselves? If adults fail to recognize that they themselves are awesome beings, full of potential and highly valued by God, how can they ever adequately appreciate God's evaluation of their children who are an extension of themselves?

Unfortunately, many of our attitudes and responses toward children are often an unconscious yet direct result of our own childhood experiences. Perhaps this lack of self-respect is a result of our own parents' projected inferiority complex; or maybe as a small child one was "brow beaten" by a teacher. Or perhaps someone remembers his own behavior in the past and will not let go of a pre-conversion estimation of himself.

Whatever the case may be, God is waiting to give forgiveness, cleansing and healing—a physical, mental and spiritual renewal—in preparation for His work in our children's lives.

A friend of ours whom we called Aunt Elaine introduced me to this type of inner healing when our daughter Paula was only two years old. After I spent several months in the hospital, Aunt Elaine, who lived some distance away from us, came to visit.

She hadn't spent too much time with Paula before she noticed something that had escaped my attention.

"This child isn't lively like a two-year-old should be," she said. "She seems sad, even a bit depressed."

Not knowing of any physical ailment, I suggested that no doubt Paula was recovering from my long absence during hospitalization.

"Well, the Lord can help *that*," she replied. "He heals memories just as He can heal anything else."

Elaine's words really encouraged me. Why not ask the Lord to heal Paula? Obviously she had suffered from loneliness and a lack of motherly attention during my hospital stay.

So that evening I discussed with my husband, Earl, what Elaine had mentioned. We decided to begin laying our hands on Paula each night as she was falling asleep, thanking the Lord for His protective care and asking Him to heal her from all hurtful memories which she could have gathered during my hospital stay. Within days she began to blossom. We continued this practice for several months until we felt that the Lord had accomplished His purposes through it—the development of a lively, radiant and joyful child.

I will forever be grateful to the Lord and to my friend for showing us not only the need but also the answer while Paula was still very young, before her personality may have become emotionally scarred.

Many of today's adults would have profited when they were yesterday's children had someone believed and prayed for their inner healing. Unfortunately, however, they never experienced the benefits of healed memories, and now as parents their own emotional hurts continue to hinder a loving, self-giving relationship with their own children.

If you are one of these individuals, I want to encourage you to believe the truth. God still loves you. God is still speaking to you. If you are a prisoner of your past, ask Him to free you. He will heal the pains of your own childhood so that you no longer need to suffer from their consequences and no longer need to inadvertently pass on this pain to others, especially your own children.

Let me illustrate how adults can thoughtlessly reproduce their own past.

I remember standing by the freezer in our mission base warehouse, pulling out frozen fish for the next day's main meal. Samuel, one of our ten-year-olds, was pulling on the big warehouse door, batting and pulling the cord that let the big door up and down. Before long another adult entered the warehouse, so intent on finding Samuel that he failed to notice me standing over to the side.

I listened silently, my heart growing heavier and heavier as the grown-up talked to Samuel. Samuel had broken faith with the singing group. He was not being faithful to the commitment he had made. According to his accuser he was being stubborn. It was not right for him to drop out of singing when the group had new performances to give.

The adult talked on and on to Samuel. But something seemed wrong. He felt that Samuel should keep on singing in that group, and he was articulating this in volumes and volumes of paragraphs. But Samuel seemed to feel differently, and he stolidly turned his face from the person, at the same time batting the cord on the warehouse door.

What was really going on? What were the real priorities? Was the adult encouraging Samuel to find out what God had in mind for him or was he choosing the easiest response—speaking and reacting from past experience? Maybe as a child he himself had been reminded of his obligations and his "stubbornness" and now he was unknowingly making incorrect deductions about Samuel and the present set of circumstances.

Later I told Eric what I had accidentally seen and heard. We decided to pray about Samuel. As we quieted our hearts for God's answer, we both felt that Samuel was to be part of the children's music-drama group. But still we were puzzled. Both of us knew that Samuel very likely was not stubborn and uncommitted as the adult leader seemed to believe. Instead we felt that Samuel might be following something deep inside himself.

"Better pray some more," Eric said. So we asked for more understanding. Eric, thirteen at this time, was Samuel's track coach and had developed a sense of responsibility for him, praying for and with him often. As a result he had boldness to ask for specifics.

"God, what do *You* want Samuel to do?" Eric perceived the answer clearly. "Be the prop man."

"Ah!" we sighed with relief and delight. It was a perfect answer. Samuel was still to be a part of the music-drama group, the King's Kids. He just was not to be singing in it anymore. He was to be the prop man instead, a responsibility I had been handling up until that time.

I was thrilled with God's idea. I knew that Samuel's eye for detail, his energy, his ability to concentrate, and his knowledge of every part of the musical play made him ideal for the job. No adult would be more careful about props, cues, and timing.

By being "stubborn" and by not letting himself be persuaded by an insistent adult, Samuel was obeying the inner voice of God's Spirit who was trying to say to him: "Yes, you are in the group, but not as a singing member. I have something else for you to do, something that just fits you in the ways you need to grow and develop for Me."

Samuel had done his part. He had heard God and had obeyed by refusing to sing anymore. But he had been stuck because he did not know how to speak out what he felt and he did not know what he was *to do*. He only knew what he was *not* to do.

"Go tell Samuel how we prayed and what you understood about him being prop man for the play," I said to Eric. "Then you two can pray about it."

I didn't see Eric again until suppertime. "What did he say?" I asked.

Eric smiled. "It fit just right," he said. "He prayed about it and it fits just right. Samuel is the prop man."

Samuel's mother agreed, and even the adult leader was willing to reconsider the matter. The responsibility fit Samuel. Prop man he became, and because he knew the songs and choreography and spoken drama lines as no nonperformer could, he was an excellent prop man for the rest of the presentations.

The point of this illustration is not that children should resist authority, but rather that those in authority are there to serve—to help the children find their place in God's plan.

God is as busy speaking to children as He is speaking to us ex-children. But we must develop sensitivity in order to hear what He is saying and see what He is doing—sensitivity toward God, toward ourselves, and toward the children.

When Earl and I were expecting our first baby, God began to show me what an awesome journey I was about to undertake. I was going to have not only the responsibility but also the privilege of introducing my child to Jesus. With God's help I was supposed to create an atmosphere wherein I could demonstrate to him or her what God is really like.

The potential for failure on my part was overwhelming. But the Holy Spirit reminded me that my lack of knowledge would become God's opportunity to teach me His way of caring.

I knew how selfish and self-centered my life had been up until that time, neglecting to do my duties, doing only what I wanted to do first. So I decided that my motherly duties would begin with breast-feeding my baby. My reasoning went like this: If I become preoccupied with my own interests, my breasts will fill up with milk and make me uncomfortable. In this way I will remember to check to see if the baby is hungry.

I'm sure this sounds strange, but I knew myself and was convinced that a bottle-fed baby might cry a long time before I became aware of it.

A friend of mine once asked me if this choice didn't result from some underlying need to do penance. Well, if we define penance as a concrete act carried out to cut across sinful habits, then I guess I would have to agree. But, nevertheless, the benefits of this strategy brought much happiness to our mother-child relationship and was the beginning of God's continued training and discipline in the art of mothering.

Two of the by-products of nursing were freedom and unwasted time. It requires perhaps ten seconds to prepare for feeding a baby and no cleaning up or storing is needed afterwards. I became aware of these benefits as the months passed. I seemed to continually have more time and mobility than the other young mothers around me.

It was some time later that I discovered the financial savings involved, as well as the psychological value of close flesh-to-flesh mothering. And others told me how important adequate sucking experience is in a child's language development and how beautifully babies are protected when they receive antibodies and additional nutrients from their mother's milk.

My decision, however, had been made in ignorance. I knew only that I was a self-centered person and I wanted to program my life so that my selfishness would not trespass upon another human being, the little infant in our family. I was learning to "do unto him as I would need to be done unto if I were his age."

This principle is the basis for all godly relationships and especially the adult-child relationship. As I began to search for ways to build an atmosphere wherein my children could develop confidence both in the expression of God's character through me and in their own worth as God's creation, I began to think about childhood—my own, my friends', and that of many of the children I had met.

I realized that basically small children love and trust themselves—that is, until through repeated failures and admonitions (which are usually given in a rather impatient and exasperated tone of voice) they are conditioned to think negatively about themselves.

Can you imagine a tiny baby seeing a rattle within his reach and then debating within himself, "Perhaps I could grab it if I tried, . . . but then again, maybe not. I might fail." Or "I might get into trouble."

Of course not. That would be ridiculous. Every healthy baby will lustily fling out a hand and grab the rattle, clutching it tightly in his fist. After all, as far as they are concerned the world is theirs. When something is there they reach for it.

We were all born this way, with a passion for life which includes reaching out and enjoying intimate touch with everything around us. We popped everything into our mouths. We screamed and made snuffling noises and burped and sighed and laughed. Sometimes we smelled bad, sometimes we smelled like talcum powder (if we were born into a culture that powdered babies).

Then when we entered the toddler stage people began to step on our toes because we were little and they did not notice us. "Ouch!" We pushed at them but they did not budge. They were preoccupied with more important matters.

No doubt we can also remember rushing home from school at one time or another, anxious to tell our mother the most thrilling thing that ever happened, only to find her occupied on the phone for endless minutes. "Oh, well," was the usual response as we went to our room and pulled out a comic book. People seemed to ignore us a lot of the time.

Recognizing this tendency of adults to ignore children (often when they need attention the most), I began to meditate on Matthew 7:12 in relationship to children: "All things whatsoever ye would that men should do to you, do ye even so to them." As I pondered Jesus' words, I began to see that a baby should not be left lying in a crib, playpen, or little hard rigid plastic container, bored and alone. He needs the fun of joining me in whatever I am doing. There are so many sounds, motions, and differing sights in my world—a world which belongs to him also.

When Eric was born one of our friends gave us a sturdy velvet baby-carrying pouch. So into the pouch he went. The pouch was fastened around my chest until he could hold his head up well, and then pouch and baby were transferred to my back. What fun it was to vacuum the floor with a baby on my back!

There were also significant by-products from this particular commitment to Eric. My hands were free to do many things: shopping, housecleaning, washing and cooking.

Of course he did not live in the pouch continually, but whenever I was ready to do something that involved a change of scenery, smell, or sound, into the pouch he went. Only gradually did I realize the benefits of close body contact, the opportunity for little eyes to search for new visual impressions and the variety and riches of sights and sounds which were stored in his unconscious self by means of this relationship. And it was all a result of reading and applying the Word of God literally.

It is the Holy Spirit speaking through the Word who can develop our sensitivity. He knows the child's needs as well as our own, and He wants to show us how to minister creatively to our children in a way which will develop their own spiritual sensitivity so they can from an early age begin to serve others.

Our part is to cooperate with Him by seriously meditating upon Scripture and completely and patiently applying it, first to ourselves and then to our children and their environment.

When Eric was a newborn, I tried to bring him into my world, into the sights and sounds of my environment. But when he began to crawl about I realized that *I* needed to enter *his* environment—his real, personal, natural environment. This extended from the floor's surface to within about sixteen inches above the floor. Consequently, whatever came within his line of vision was quite different from my visual environment. While he could gaze at the underside of the table, I saw only its topside. I wanted to get into his environment and experience it, so one morning I decided to get down where he was.

I noted the height of his eyes from the surface of the floor, which was about eight inches. Then I tried to position my own eyes at exactly the same level. This entailed lying flat on the floor. What a way to take a tour: living room, dining room, and kitchen. I took in everything possible— sights, textures, temperatures and sounds.

The results were fascinating. His space, his environment, was extremely interesting visually but extremely boring tactually and audially. So I began to add items to his environment: pie pans that would make a delicious clamor if he bumped them while crawling, an empty oatmeal box which could easily roll back and forth, some fabric and a few other objects which I would have liked "done unto me" down there on the floor.

As Eric grew older there were more problems to be answered. How could I arrange his environment so that he could make his own bed at the age of two? I knew he had an inner urge to accomplish this feat; but was it really practical? Could he actually be trained to do this task? My husband and I looked at catalogues with pictures of this low bed and that low bed, all too expensive. And to get a good firm mattress required extra money besides. At last the answer dawned upon us: a twelve-dollar, lavender-and-green plaid sleeping bag from Sears.

The sleeping bag stayed, jelly-roll fashion, against his bedroom wall all day, used by him as a wonderful sit-down place, a sort of couch. At bedtime he simply unrolled it. This took about thirty seconds and then voila, instant bed! Obviously anyone twenty-six inches tall can make up his own bed if it is nice and bulky and rolls.

A checklist of Eric's "sleeping-bag" benefits are as follows:

- ☑ He was able to do it himself.
- ☑ His actions included the possibility of choice: do I roll it or unroll it; shall I do it fast or slow? Shall I drag it to this side of the room or to the other for tonight? etc.
- ☑ A sleeping bag on a carpeted floor provided quite adequate firmness.
- ☑ The cost was reasonable.
- ☑ It was very washable.

Besides these benefits, the rolled-up sleeping bag provided empty floor space for block-building and tumbling. For the next four years his room contained little except for that bag, a couple of brick-and-board shelves for his current interest materials, and a box for stuffed things. There was also a very large painted cardboard box he used as a house. I had cut doors and windows out of it and he could move it about from room to room.

His clothes were kept in a small chest of drawers in his closet. He worked out his own way of storing his clothes, and since it was his own affair I do not even remember what the arrangement was. But one thing I do remember—oh! the glorious space.

Space means as much to a little child as it does to an adult. We all need space to move in, to build in, and to be in. We need space to create in and space to make decisions about. That space cost Earl and me nothing. We merely removed the hindrances to the space that already existed.

Actually, that is what sensitivity is all about—making "space" for the child, giving him room to develop as a unique personality under the care of the Holy Spirit. Who would have guessed how influential even our sleeping bag philosophy was at exposing our children to more of the Holy Spirit's work in their lives?

The sleeping bag proved very adaptable. It fit into almost any area, and as a result sleeping-bag-plus-space equaled home. I soon became known in various prayer, fellowship, and Bible-study groups around town as the "lady with the lavender blanket." No matter where we went in those days, we had the sleeping bag for one child and a big lavender blanket for the other. The children rolled up in their bag and blanket under our chairs during the meetings, and whether sleeping or awake, prayer and thanksgiving flowed around them. No wonder Eric and Paula knew our Lord as their Lord at the ages of four and three.

Not only had we reproduced physical children, but with

the help of the Lord we had brought forth a brother and sister in Christ.

You may not be able to use a sleeping bag and lavender blanket in your own situation, but I encourage you to creatively develop ways with your own children of "doing unto" them as you would have done to you if you were their size and age.

As we leave the decade of the seventies and the "ME" generation behind us, we as Christian parents have the opportunity of making the eighties a time when the "We" generation prevails: a generation in which adults and children begin to know each other in the Spirit—sharing, working and worshipping together—sensitive to the lordship of Jesus Christ.

3. Slow-Baked Cookies

"Mama, we've invented a cookie!" Paula excitedly told me one day.

"*I* invented the cookie we invented," Eric corrected her.

"Well, I helped with your invention," Paula replied, determined to have her share of the glory.

"Tell me about the cookie," I said. I knew that people make up recipes for cookies, but I had never heard about the *invention* of a cookie.

They grinned. My response was just what they had hoped for—interest and an eagerness to sample their wares.

"We won't give you one now," they continued. "We're saving them for you and the company."

I paused. Did I dare trust their taste buds? Would we be able to down what they presented to us? After all, they were only five and seven years old. Although Eric had been cooking since he was four, I still considered a child's three-year repertoire of cooking experience limited.

How would I handle the potential social blunder? What if the guests felt obliged to eat the children's invention? Would I find myself being thought of as a mother who dotingly foists the products of her children's inexpert hands off on others? Quickly I began to stall for time.

"Do you have enough cookies for everyone?" I asked Eric, all the while trying to formulate an answer to the situation which would not only save face for me but which would also encourage the children's creativity and their desire to serve.

The children ran into the other room to count the cookies, and then returned. "Yes," they said. "We have enough cookies for everyone to have two or three."

"Did you clean up your mess?" I was still trying to make a decision.

"No."

"Well, clean up your mess, and then I'll see."

I had several things to do before the guests arrived, and I forgot about the cookies. Before long it was late afternoon and four or five guests arrived for conversation and a cup of tea. We were all engrossed in a stimulating discussion when I noticed someone munching on a hearty-looking cookie. It was about three or four inches in diameter. Quickly I glanced around the circle of friends. The children had already made the rounds, quietly offering each guest a cookie, served from a nicely washed cookie tin. They were just then coming around to me.

I took one bite. It was delicious! Soon I heard Margarita saying to Eric, "And you invented this? Can you tell me your recipe?

"Of course," he said, and he started off, "You need cinnamon—"

"Wait, wait," she said. "I need my pencil." She dug around in her purse until she found her pencil and notebook. Then she wrote down his invention. I could not hear their conversation because of the chatter around me, so I asked Eric for the recipe after the guests had gone.

When we got to the part which dealt with oven temperature I suddenly realized that they had turned on the oven without adult supervision. So I reprimanded them for this.

Eric stared at the floor. "Well, I didn't turn it on high," he explained. "Only to 200°."

That, I suppose, explained part of their delicious taste—a long, slow bake in the oven at half the usual cookie-baking temperature.

"You must not turn on the oven without a grown-up. So you've got to promise me not to do it again."

"Okay. But it was a surprise for you, you know."

"Yes, I know. And they were scrumptious. Thank you."

That night as I got ready for bed I had to chuckle. I could see it all again—Margarita writing down Eric's description of his cookie invention as if she were getting a prized recipe from another adult. I wondered if he had told her about the 200-degree baking temperature. I figured he hadn't. Too bad, I thought. Her cookies could never come out the same as the children's. A long, slow bake was the secret of the cookie invention's deliciousness.

Children's growth is likewise slow. God invented children. He knows all their component parts, and His Spirit is actively involved in their developmental processes—processes which cannot be rushed. We need to follow God's clock, and not devise our own timetables.

God in His wisdom establishes individual growth patterns—"recipes," if you will—for each child, and we parents need to follow the instructions. In the same way that each cooking recipe is arranged in steps which are often dependent upon each other, so also a child's social, physical, and spiritual development is arranged in successive steps. As a result they can move smoothly and successfully through their current developmental stage only when they have successfully grown through the preceding stages.

Therefore as parents we need to avoid frustrating our children by expecting them to act younger or older than they are. Remember what the Apostle Paul said in Ephesians 6:4: "Fathers, do not provoke your children to anger, but bring them up in the discipline [training] and instruction of the Lord."

Young parents today are easily discouraged by such admonishing words. Often they themselves were not parented well.

At no time should we allow ourselves to become discouraged. God is Lord over all things, including our, and our children's, sins and failures. We need a "bigger picture of

Jesus,'' as some YWAM friends would say, whenever we are overcome by doubt about our ability to teach our children, to instruct them in the Lord.

Take time to consider the greatness of our God. He rules over all things. We have yet to see the complete extension of His loving rule over the rebel forces within man and within the spiritual realm. But He is waiting, patiently, for each of us to agree to His sovereignty so He can bless us and make us all what we were created to be.

Take heart in the midst of the troubles your child is causing you. Let each incident that arises between you bring you to your knees in prayer. We talk too much and pray too little. We discuss and complain and ''share with others'' what ought to be taken straight to the Lord for His correction and His insights for us.

He may even surprise you by saying, ''You're doing a good job,'' when you're convinced of the contrary. And frequently, very frequently as you are starting out under His lordship, He will say, ''Go ask the child to forgive *you* and pray for *you.*'' This was my experience in our early years together. We would ''hit the floor'' regularly, as we called it when kneeling seemed the only way to express deep contrition, and Eric or Paula would earnestly ask the Lord to ''forgive Mama, please, for getting mad at us'' or ''for forgetting to keep her promise'' or whatever the transgression might be. I asked for forgiveness faithfully, seemingly unendingly. With children, forgiveness is to be quickly asked for, and quickly given. The children never had much time to build up barriers. We were all too busy repenting, receiving and giving forgiveness, and enjoying the resulting joy of the Lord.

And take courage to assert your leadership. Your role is crucial to the child's development. *You* are the most important ingredient in your child's whole life, besides the Lord himself. The child *cannot* know the faithfulness and steadfast trustworthiness of our God if we are as firm as wet macaroni whenever the child decides to set himself against us. It takes humility to ask for forgiveness when we have sinned. And it takes equal humility to stand firm and insist upon obedience from the child when he is defiant and has decided to test his limits with you. You must win over him, and you must win out every time, when it comes to a test of wills, or his confidence in your strength and judgment will erode very quickly. But you cannot make this firm stand and stick with it if unresolved sin habits are plaguing you. That is why hearty, ongoing repentance precedes strong stands and firm action in our parenting. Lots of the usual "strong stands" parents feel they have to make would never have been necessary anyway if parents had not provoked a child to his rebellion or had perhaps not neglected early pleas for help that finally turned to frustrated shouts of defiance.

Did you know that God sees all things, including our quarrels with our children? There is no need to be embarrassed. We need to get down on our knees together. He will always do far more for us than we know how to ask Him in the explosion times. He takes us at our word and clears up the present concern, and then cleverly makes the most out of our morsels of humility to work deep changes in us besides. Let us thank Him, that He does *not* let us go on in self-destructive and child-destructive ways! He looks out for His precious creatures, us *and* them. He is Lord.

Though He will help us de-fuse their anger when we provoke them, we need to know what angers children. Impoliteness does. Neglect does. Failing to keep our promises to them grieves them seriously. Misunderstanding them and their intentions and their abilities to perform what we think they should be able to perform hurts them.

A child can most easily be provoked to anger and frustration when he is continually living under expectations and demands which he cannot physically or emotionally fulfill. God has wisely put an internal clock or biological timetable in each child which often enables him to know what is going on inside himself better than we do as outsiders trying to "look in."

Perhaps this concept can be better understood if I tell you about the "chewing sponges" era at our household.

Thumb-sucking became an item of contention between Paula and me when she was four years old. After all, four is not three or two, and I did not enjoy watching her slurp on the tasty digit. I figured she had had enough sucking practice. So I tried to negotiate with her. It seemed, however, that she felt she still had a real need to suck on something. My problem then was to find a suitable substitute for her thumb. I wanted to satisfy her need to suck sufficiently, but I did not want her to develop another addiction.

Finally I had an idea. Sponges! The synthetic kind. They are squishy but firm. The corner of one would fit nicely into her mouth. To keep them clean, I decided to buy a set of them and put them in various parts of the house, at least one per room, so that she would never be without one. They would stay in their designated place in each area except when in her mouth and thus would not be dragged around here and there, lost, dropped or in other ways be subjected to dirt.

I suppose I had in mind a sort of genteel nibbling at a sponge when the urge to chew or suck came on her, like a lady at a bon-bon dish. So after buying the sponges, Paula and I talked the matter over and I placed them in their various locales. She seemed quite taken with the idea. The sponges chewed nicely, she said, and tasted all right. The colors were pretty and she seemed quite happily impressed with the trouble I was going to to satisfy her needs. I in turn was happily impressed with her interest and enthusiasm and thought we had met the enemy and conquered him through this heretofore unknown device to stop thumb-sucking.

But before long, the sponges began to gather dust. The

one in the den I especially noticed. It was a dainty pink and, located on the bottom shelf of the end table, it was visible from every direction.

Week after week it greyed. I dusted around and under it from time to time. Months passed. It was a delicate situation. I did not like to inquire about her personal use of the sponges throughout the house. I really couldn't tell that any had been used.

Then the day came when I ran out of household cleaning sponges. Instead of waiting to buy more I used her pink sponge to clean something. Then gradually and secretively I used up the rest of the sponges, one by one. I didn't think she was even noticing until one day I heard her talking with Aunt Elaine. Elaine had asked her why she was still sucking her thumb, to which she replied, "Because Mama has used up all my sponges."

Faith had been broken. Her property had been confiscated. Needless to say it was hard to explain to Aunt Elaine both the original project and my sponge-snatching from a needy child.

Later I talked to Paula about the sponges. I reminded her that it had been months since I first bought the sponges and I was sure she hadn't used any of them.

"Yes, I know," she answered, "but you never can tell when I might start. And now I can't because you've taken all my sponges and used them up."

Then I got very basic with her. "Listen," I said, "I don't like to look at you sucking your thumb. You have to live with me. What are you going to do about it?"

"I'll stop on my fifth birthday."

"If you can decide to stop on your fifth birthday, you can decide to stop now," I said.

"No, I can't. But I will stop on my birthday. You'll see."

"I don't believe it."

"That's okay. You'll see."

I continued in my unbelief. After all, wasn't it just a

matter of the will? But Paula went serenely on her way, sucking her thumb, unperturbed by my evident doubt.

Finally her birthday arrived. And Paula stopped sucking her thumb without regression and without difficulty. I do not understand it. All I know is that I analyzed the situation incorrectly. I had expected her to demonstrate self-control in an area which neither she nor I fully understood. Somehow, though, she was able to perceive the timing built into her.

God is never in such a rush as we are, particularly in relationship to our children. They become complete in a function only when all the aspects and the skills necessary to that function have been perfectly developed and are ready to be joined—joined in that mysterious "fullness of time" which cannot be precisely predicted. These sensitive points, i.e., the coming together of developed abilities in order to create a faculty, are delicate in the extreme and must be treated as such, with care and with consideration.

Do you remember when you first said, "Now you're a big boy! You can do it by yourself"? Grown-ups often use this phrase when the child has done something that shows his newly developing coordination. We like to watch them develop from this skill to the next—for example, from crawling to walking. Walking without anyone holding his hand marks a tremendously important day for the small child.

Another big moment is the time when a child begins to talk. What was his first word? Everyone is interested in this.

Then comes the day when he loses his first tooth. This is another important day for the child. Many of them find it hard to believe that another tooth will ever grow in to take the missing tooth's place. The wait seems so long.

Waiting is often difficult for parents as well. In an industrialized society so conscious of achievement and production, even parents can unknowingly begin to evaluate their children by how fast they are growing and how much they are achieving, failing to realize the child's need to just "be."

Their development, physically and spiritually, cannot be scheduled. It is not subject to force and extreme control. If we employ these tactics, our own children will be subject to unbearable frustration.

Instead we must be ready to help where needed, anticipating the rough places and guiding from a short distance. Then we can sit back, confident that the real "Director" is in charge.

Perhaps your child plays a musical instrument and you have attended his orchestra concert. Each child involved has spent time practicing his own instrument and now they all have the same piece of music before them. But only the conductor can bring it all together to produce the desired harmony. It doesn't just happen. It has been planned for and worked at. We the audience merely enjoy the beautiful music because of the decisions and refined discernment of that orchestra leader.

In the same way God is coordinating and overseeing the development of each child. Not only is He using the "slow-baked" method, but He has also determined what the basic ingredients are for each child. These ingredients are found to some degree in every child and should be nurtured and preserved at any cost.

The first ingredient or characteristic of childhood is humility. Jesus put much emphasis on this aspect of the child. Matthew 18:3-4 says, "Unless you turn and become like children you will never enter the kingdom of heaven. Whoever humbles himself like this child, he is the greatest in the kingdom of heaven."

Again in Luke 18:17 Jesus said, "Whoever does not receive the kingdom of God like a child shall not enter it." This verse is set in the context of a discussion on humility. It is preceded by the parable of the Pharisee and the Publican and followed by the story of the rich young ruler. Jesus is saying that humility cuts across "who" you are and "what" you have.

What better example could Jesus have picked for demonstrating the true meaning of humility? A young child has not accomplished anything that would bring him status in the world's point of view. He just *is*. Neither does he possess anything that has not been given to him.

Instead, a child starts life out loving and admiring his parents. He wants to be like them, helping them, giving of himself to them and working like them. Parents who refuse their humble efforts have been later heard to say in regret, "I wish I had let Sally wash dishes when she was little. She really wanted to then. Now when she is old enough to do the dishes [in the parent's estimation], she no longer wants to. Before she thought of dishes as fun. Now it is drudgery."

Another characteristic of a child is a quiet persistence in whatever he is doing. When Paula was two and a half she attended her first "school." This school made use of the Montessori method and played an integral part in Paula's development. In the classroom there was an irresistible item: a sturdy child-sized ironing board and a small electric iron. This was used to teach very small children how to iron napkins. During her first two months of school, however, Paula spent almost all of her time watching little squares of cotton cloth drying on a clothesline.

The reason? Step number one in ironing was to sprinkle your "to-be-ironed" napkins to just the right dampness for ironing. But sprinkling with the little sprinkling bottle was in itself such a fascinating sensation that she daily sprinkled her little store of napkins to dripping sogginess and then pinned them on the children's clothesline to hang till they were absolutely dry again. It usually took all morning for them to dry.

Patiently she watched them dry, then put them away, to be sprinkled again the next morning since there was no time left to sprinkle them again that day. Patience and persistence cannot be measured in the usual school-testing processes, but nevertheless, these qualities prove to be necessities both in physical and spiritual development.

Romans 5:4 says that "endurance produces character" and it is "character [that] produces hope." In a day when Christian parents and others as well are beginning to wonder what hope there is for their child's future, we need to protect and encourage the seeds of patience and persistence which God has put into our children. We need to pray about these areas of our children's lives and cooperate with the Holy Spirit in practical avenues for developing these character qualities.

Little squares of cotton cloth, clothespins on a low clothesline and a "real-life" iron for children are nothing in themselves but when used to enlarge Godlike qualities within an eternal soul they are worth their weight in gold. Thank God for adults who recognize a child's need for real work.

Another beautiful quality about children is their simplicity. Children think in terms of basics. Paula was only four years old when she drew my attention to this fact. It had been our family custom that whenever someone's birthday arrived, we would have special prayer for them. So on my birthday I was made to sit on a chair as the rest of the family gathered around me to pray.

When Paula's turn came she placed her hands on my arm and prayed, "Thank you, God, that Mama exists." It was a short, simple prayer, not soon forgotten. Someone thanked God I existed, someone who knew me very, very well. I was affirmed in a deeply fundamental way.

Children see things in their simplest fundamental forms. Their simple directness is a precious gift of God to us. May we treat this quality with respect and stand in awe at the love God shows to us through it. What if we went on, heedless and unthankful for a small person's care and concern for us?

Prompt, expressive thankfulness is also a child characteristic. The smallest child is full of thanksgiving. Children thank us with smiles, chatter, or maybe even a piece of string from out of some special secret treasure store of their own. They kiss us and, grinning, give us some inky handprints on a piece of paper, or make us a peculiarly green cake on our birthday. And we receive their gifts with a catch in our hearts. They give freely, from out of themselves.

When a child values his own life and what God is doing in it, he also values the lives of others. He becomes sensitive to others' needs. This sensitivity is often seen in quiet, unobtrusive service.

Have you ever been really, really, really tired? I have. When Paula was very young she would slip off my shoes and socks, so subtly that I was almost oblivious to her action. She would rub and rub my feet until I felt refreshed again. Only after many minutes did I perceive her tender service. It was always so gently and unobtrusively done that it barely penetrated my conscious awareness. This was her expression of the art of footwashing (see the Gospel of John, chapter 13) practiced to near perfection.

Sensitivity to another's needs can lead the child into some detailed plotting, like the "let's make a picnic for Jackie" event.

Eric was twelve when he decided that Jackie, one of the helpers in the King's Kids program, needed some plain old-fashioned fun. Jackie had been spending extra time and effort on rehearsals and performances that year, even though she was not feeling too well, and as a result she was becoming increasingly tired.

Seeing this, Eric planned a picnic just for the two of them. When he checked with me I agreed that it sounded like a worthwhile idea, but I did not have any extra food to give him for the picnic.

"Oh, that's all right," he said. "I've got some allowance money left. I'll go to the store by myself," he emphasized, "and get all we need. Just let me use your picnic basket." Reflecting for a moment, he asked, "Is there anything else I need to take along?"

I suggested a quilt for sitting on the ground.

"That's great!"

Off he went to the store to buy his choice of foods. When he returned his arms were full. He had figured out how much he himself could eat and had safely multiplied the quantity by two or maybe three. I hoped he knew how hungry she was! I didn't ask him how much he had spent, but it looked like he had used up all he had for the picnic. I sighed and mentally made a note to be ready to advance him a small sum when his sister's birthday came around shortly.

As he unloaded his grocery bag I noticed various kinds of cheese and crackers, meat, fruits, and even pickles. He stored it carefully in the refrigerator, labeling each brown paper bag with his name. I put aside the basket as he had requested and got out the quilt.

Unknowingly Eric was living out his life according to an Old Testament principle: "You shall rejoice in all the good which the Lord your God has given to you and to your house" (Deut. 26:11). This principle defines a very basic attitude which we need to return to as families.

God means that we are to be not only thankful for all the good that He has given us but we are also to rejoice in it, to have fun with it together as families. Though our "good" be little or much, God has always intended that relationships within the family and with God be a source of rejoicing and fun. And children in particular can minister "fun" in our relationships if we cooperate with them, recognizing that God desires to express himself even in this area.

A tired but smiling Jackie followed Eric into our apartment after their picnic together. "It was great!" she said to me. "Just what I needed! How did Eric know what would perk me up?"

I smiled and shrugged. Who knows how they know? They just do. Three cheers for lavish picnics, little songs, and thankful prayers for our existence!

Eric had been building guitars with his carpenter tools. He used boards, nails, and strong rubber bands.

"Look, Ma," he said to me one day while I was washing dishes. He showed me a well-made, two-string plucking instrument. It had a square of wood placed under the two rubber band strings in the center of the square sounding board. The small wood square had nails sticking up at each corner. The square itself was firmly nailed into the sounding board through its center with one nail. But yet, with a turn of the hand, he could turn the square, making the nails touch and stretch the rubber band strings, thus producing much variety in pitch and even timbre. It was quite a piece of work.

"It's my unicorn," he said.

"Why did you name it unicorn?"

"Because it has two strings."

This was too much to take without comment! "Uni means one," I said.

"No, uni means two. And I named it a unicorn because it has two strings."

"Uni means one. I can show you in the dictionary." This was a ridiculous statement because he was just four and could not read yet.

"Uni means two." And with that, he went on about his work, building a balalaika-looking guitar next.

What was there to say? Nothing. I thought about it a lot. *Did* uni mean two, at least sometimes? At least when naming a remarkable two-stringed guitar? And maybe also when one is an infant, still tied up close in the nursing relationship? After all, he had first known himself while he was still a partner in a twosome. A child's world always consists of himself and somebody else. Perhaps that is why he, like God, is creative. He desires to create extensions of himself. "One" is a very sterile number. The number two has far more potential. It includes the possibilities of love and sharing, understanding and giving of oneself.

When the child is small his mother is all in all to him. She is his light, his fount of wisdom, his source of supply, his private mode of entertainment. She tells him he is helpful, big, neat, thoughtful, kind or patient, depending upon his response in differing situations. He defines himself in her terms.

And if during this time his self-image is enhanced by character-building compliments, his creativity will burst forth in innumerable ways as he discovers new things and new aspects about himself. Only as he discovers himself in relation to God, though, can he fully cooperate with the creative urges within himself—urges which will bring forth much praise and appreciation of life and relationship itself.

This type of appreciation is often demonstrated through singing. At three years of age Paula sat on a stool singing while I ironed clothes. The song to God went on and on. She sang of Zacchaeus' life and then came the refrain: "You are so good, so good to me, And so polite, And Jesus too . . . " On and on she sang, twenty, thirty verses for twenty or thirty minutes. She sang this each day for several days while I ironed.

Every so often I was tempted to say, "That's enough now," but I hesitated. It would be so easy to grieve the Holy Spirit in a little child. For it is He who urges them to participate in life according to God's desires. "Sing to him [the Lord], sing praises to him, tell of all his wonderful works" (1 Chron. 16:9).

Paula truly was telling of His wonderful works as she sang her song. It sprang from her heart because she was experiencing the joy of relationship between herself and God. She knew that God was so "good" and so "polite" and she appreciated that.

We as parents need to emulate these qualities. Let's not only be good to our children, but polite also, never forgetting that they are special. God has invented the "recipe" for each one and the instructions read—"Bake slowly to avoid burning."

4. Like Father, Like Son

"You're a chip off the old block!" Edmund Burke, the 18th-century British statesman and orator, first used this phrase to describe William Pitt, his contemporary and prime minister. He meant to say that William Pitt, the son, was made of the same stuff as his father, William Pitt, the first Earl of Chatham. Both men had pursued a life of service to their country and government.

Today, however, the phrase usually has humorous overtones. And as a result the depth of truth hidden in these words is often overlooked.

Children are indeed made out of the same stuff as their parents. And we as parents cannot expect our children to be spiritually more than we are willing to be ourselves.

When God first created Adam, "he made him in the likeness of God" (Gen. 5:1), without sin. Then, "when Adam had lived a hundred and thirty years, he became the father of a son *in his own likeness*" (Gen. 5:3). By that time Adam and Eve had fallen and they could reproduce only after their own kind, both physically and spiritually impaired.

This principle of reproduction has held true for each successive generation. Were it not for specific intervention on God's part into human history, there is no way of knowing how far mankind would have strayed from the original model. Cain was only one generation removed from Adam when he tried to please God through his own understanding and in his own way.

We see the same problem today. Christian parents and

other adults are trying to guide successive generations into right understanding of and right relationship to God without being intimately acquainted with the original designer themselves.

Jeremiah 9:23-24 says, "Let not the wise man glory in his wisdom, let not the mighty man glory in his might, let not the rich man glory in his riches; but let him who glories glory in this, *that he understands and knows me*, that I am the Lord who practice steadfast love, justice and righteousness in the earth; for in these things I delight, says the Lord."

To the very young child the "image" of God is his parents. And as he grows older, even though he begins to relate to God and the truth of Scripture, he sometimes has a hard time differentiating between the example of his parents and his understanding of what God is really like. Children, even very young ones, sense who we really are, not who or what we say we are.

In order to bring our life attitudes and life-style into line with our "words," we need to saturate ourselves in Scripture continually. Then we will better understand God's character and His methods of dealing with us—the same character and methods He wishes us to employ in relation to our children.

On the night before His crucifixion, Jesus summarized His whole earthly ministry with these words: "I am among you as one who serves" (Luke 22:27). We older brothers and sisters are to be among the children as those who serve. We are to help them enter into their spiritual inheritance.

Let's consider what is involved. A good servant anticipates needs and seeks to meet those needs before they are even consciously recognized by the person being ministered to. He never says, "I will serve this way, but I will not serve that way." Instead, His service is appropriate to the situation and the specific individual involved.

By now you are no doubt asking, "Who can be all that?"

Obviously only Jesus can. But "to this *you* have been
called, because Christ also suffered for you, leaving you an
example, that you should follow in his steps" (1 Pet. 2:21).

Let's study our example more closely. What were the
qualities which made Jesus such a good servant?

First of all He was gentle. A gentle person is patient and
mild, never violent, harsh or rough. He knows that the
"wrath of man does not accomplish the righteousness of
God."

One day when I had a room full of two-year-olds at nursery school, Cathy was a grumpy little menace all morning
long. Finally I took her out to the hall for a drink of water.

"Cathy," I asked, "how do you feel today?" She continued to glare at me with angry eyes and pouting lips. "Do
you *know* how you feel?" I continued. She shook her head.

Cathy had been disrupting the class long enough, and I
was becoming impatient. Sensing my need, I quickly asked
the Holy Spirit for help. As I stood looking at Cathy, I suddenly felt the urge to try another approach.

"Cathy, do you *want* to feel the way you are feeling?"
She shook her head. This was important. Sometimes Cathy
liked to be mad. Sometimes she liked to stay mad. But this
was different. Things seemed to be out of her control, and
being harsh or impatient with her would only have compli-
cated the situation. Instead, I decided to try out what I felt
she could do to help herself.

"Cathy," I said to her, "say, 'Jesus.' "

She said it.

"Can you say it again?"

She said it again.

"Now try saying this: 'I belong to Jesus.' " I could ask
her to do this because even though she was only two and a
half, she had previously told Jesus she wanted to be "His
girl." She knew about Him. And she was used to hearing us
talk about Him and to Him every day.

So, it didn't seem strange or untruthful to me to have

her say out loud, "I belong to Jesus." She had said the same thing in her own words previously as she participated in our group activities. So I felt I was merely getting her to reaffirm the relationship she had already established with Him.

"All right," I said. "Now whenever you feel like you are feeling now, just say, 'Jesus. Jesus.' Then say, 'I belong to Jesus.' Can you do that?"

She nodded her head. I had her repeat the statements over several times. She sighed and within seconds she was no longer upset. The powerful yet gentle name of Jesus had done more in a few minutes than I could ever have done with all my natural strength or forceful disposition. What treasures of truth are at our disposal if only we would begin to apply them to our relationships.

The second quality which made Jesus such a good servant was persistence. A persistent person refuses to give up, especially when he is faced with opposition or difficulty.

Can you imagine where many of us would be today had the Lord given up on us after our first, second, or perhaps third refusal to repent and accept His love? Truly "love bears all things, believes all things, hopes all things, endures all things" (1 Cor. 13:7).

Bang was a child who understood and experienced this type of love. She had lost her father the previous year. He had died of leukemia—a young missionary, a young father and husband. Bang was a solemn-eyed seven-year-old, but bright and possessed with great personal dignity.

Bang won an Easter-egg drawing contest the year I knew her—a contest sponsored by a local store. Her drawing had resurrection power—a certain whiteness and brightness exploding through her childish design. When we made kites and decorated them, Bang's kite displayed the same style of design. It was full of joy and confidence in the love and power of God, who keeps us on this side or on the other side of death.

Supported by her mother's prayers, tears and faith as

her steadfast help, Bang worked her way through to victory that year. Neither she nor her mother had given in to self-pity. She did not have questions. She had confidence. She had come to know a personal God who loved her and nurtured her, a God who would not forsake her even when life was extremely difficult.

The third quality of Jesus which we need to emulate is consistency. A consistent person conducts himself in harmony with his beliefs and profession. As a Christian, I had always known that God was truth, but especially when the children were small, I became determined to speak the truth to them in love and nothing beyond the truth. What an exercise in vocabulary, logic and diction! What a crucible for creating self-control and patience! If one of them hit the other, I would say, "It hurts when you're hit. It will hurt a while. Then it will stop hurting." This was plain, unadorned truth. The usual adult comments, "Oh, he didn't mean to hurt you," and "There, there, it's not that bad," and "Oh, I'm so sorry you got hurt. There, there, it won't hurt long," were replaced by speaking the truth.

Besides being a step in the development of consistency in my own life, "speaking the truth" gave both the children and me an amazing respect for the adequate use of language in our relationship. I also noticed that giving a name (it had to be an accurate name) to a feeling, process, or thought within the child seemed to make him stand taller. He would draw in his breath, put his chest out, and seem to increase in dignity and stature. Perhaps this was because he was no longer groping around with the unknown but had through naming the feeling or process gained understanding in handling himself.

God of course relates to us in the same way. He wants to help us to develop our full potential in the Holy Spirit. That's why He explains things to us. The whole Bible is a centuries-long project in explaining things.

When Adam and Even sinned God came to them immediately, not just to see what they had done (He already knew that), but seeking to help them recover. God is never the type who says, "Well, you've made your bed; now you'll have to lie in it." Instead, He lovingly shows us what we've done wrong and what can be done to rectify the situation.

The blood sacrifice of Jesus was carefully explained to the people through the elaborate Tabernacle and sacrificial system which God set up through Moses. Most of the people, however, were so absorbed in the detailed enactment of God's explanation that they seemed to overlook the true meaning. Nevertheless, it was unmistakable to the people that God was saying something extremely important. He had written it in so large a measure upon their customs, culture, and history. God wants to explain things to us also.

In his first year in high school Eric was praying about the priorities God had for him at school, particularly with relationship to extra-curricular activities. Eric was very desirous to influence his peer group toward his Saviour.

The idea of joining the Orators Club was one thought that came up during his prayer time. But why Orators Club? God explained why at the beginning of the next school year, several months later.

"If you want to take the whole land [the high school] for Me," explained the Lord, "take the giants." Athletics and Orators Club were clearly two giants in the school program. That's why God had said that if Eric wanted to be a territory invader for the Lord Jesus, he was to take on the giants first.

If we are going to be like our Father-God in relation to our children, we must not only take on His disposition but we must also be concerned about the things He is concerned about. If God thinks it is important to explain things to His children, then we must make "explanations" a regular part of our interaction with our own children.

No doubt you've heard parents say, "I don't have to explain it to you. Just do as I say."

Although there may be instances when a child is belligerantly demanding an explanation in order to avoid obeying, I think most of the time their questions come from an inquisitive nature and an honest desire to understand. Somehow they feel that if they thoroughly understand a request, it makes it much easier to obey. Psychologically explanations are valuable also. When a person takes time to patiently explain something to a child, he is in effect saying, "You are valuable, I trust you, and I'm not trying to lord it over you."

Another of God's concerns is our defense. Physically and spiritually He has built many defense mechanisms into our bodies. Our sense of pain, our antibody system, our sensitivity to injustice, and our ability to discern discrepancies between what is and what ought to be are all obvious examples of His desire to protect us. We are His creation and He has an active and fierce commitment to our defense.

The little children are "our creation" and deserve this same type of commitment from us. In an age of increasing abortion, when children are no longer safe even within their own mothers' bodies, we need to reexamine not our individual rights according to the Constitution but our personal responsibilities according to the Word of God.

The nature of childhood itself tells us that they need to be defended. Children are weak and helpless and the world is a very big place.

Fortunately, however, there are some adults who recognize the children's need to be defended. I remember a very large religious conference on the ministry of the small child. Although it was almost a thousand-mile trip, the group leading the teaching had decided to take their small children along with them to the conference. These folks felt that it was important to give team teaching, and the children's presence was important in that setting.

Arriving early they set up a small mobile demonstration center where the children could interact in the same environment as they did in the home community.

It was an informal-looking affair, though carefully prayed through and worked out. Boxes and boards made shelves. Chairs formed barriers to create the space the children would have for themselves.

Then came the adults to hear the teaching. The little children were already there, with their things in the space set aside for them. The grown-ups began to fill up the room. They took the chairs. They pushed back the shelving. The children's things were pushed aside. Soon the little ones were against the wall with no space to move and no space to get at their work.

The community that had come to teach was very polite. They did not push anyone out of the area. But finally one of them stood up and said, "You have pushed the children aside. You have taken the space they need. And this is what we want you to learn to repent about."

It was eloquent. And it was unforgettable. The adults should have limited their "right" to sit anywhere they chose in order for the little children to move about freely and interact comfortably.

This incident reminded me once again that the dignity and value which God has placed upon human life and especially upon little children is not readily accepted by the natural man. The defense of "life" is a spiritual principle and can be learned only from the Holy Spirit.

He is our teacher and life is our schoolroom. And His qualifications are beyond compare. He never gives us a piece of information and then expects us to figure out what to do with it ourselves. Instead, as Lord both of the individuals and their circumstances, He applies the truth to us in our circumstances, staying with us and personally supervising our "journey" through life.

As we go from here to there along a timeline, He makes it happen. A journey has a beginning, a duration, and an end.

And it is His business to explain the things that will get us safely through the journey. He never leads us in circles but accomplishes specific purposes through each step of the journey.

We are something precious that He is developing and growing and taking along a path, and we must be defended constantly if we are to make it to the path's end. Every step moves us into new and unknown territory. And, He would not go to all this trouble—His explanations, His defense of us—unless we were very special to Him. Obviously our journey is very important.

And so is the journey we are taking with our children. It is not enough to tell them scriptural principles; we must live them out with them, helping them to apply truth to their circumstances. This involves time. There is no substitute for time spent with our children, talking with them, listening to them, working and playing together. Time is the common denominator in all of our journeys—a factor which is meant to develop not so much our "doing" as our "being"—being like Him.

First John 3:2 says, "Beloved, we are God's children now; it does not yet appear what we shall be, but we know that when he appears we shall be like him. . . . " For the present, however, John says, "We are God's children now." And this fact is reason enough for God to respect us. He has an immense capacity to respect—even persons and things which we might consider despicable. He treats us as persons worthy of attention even when we are still grimy and marred by sin. His is a concentrated constant attention of the positive sort.

We must learn to give this same positive attention and respect to our children. To better understand what respect is let's make an acrostic.

R stands for "recognition." Unless we are willing to recognize God's Spirit working in and through the child we will never be able to respect him in the way God wants us to. We need to consider in great depth and detail what God is doing in their lives and what He is telling us to do for them, and with them, and on behalf of them. They are not to become replicas of ourselves. They are to become unique creations. Neither they nor we know what they are to be, because it has not yet come to pass. But God knows. They are in process, and He knows the outcome of the process and is indeed in control of the process.

Let the *E* of respect stand for "expression." Respect is not just something we feel but something we do. We need to express respect for the child. This can be as simple as giving them the usual courteous speech we would give to a stranger or a visitor. For example, I have often been embarrassed when an adult who is talking to me suddenly changes his tone of voice or choice of words when he turns to speak to his child.

Why should children be subjected to a low-grade, discourteous type of speech? If what Jesus said about the kingdom of heaven belonging to children is really true, then they are very important persons and should be treated that way. There can never be respect without courtesy.

The *S* of respect stands for "silence." Most of us have been taught that when we are with people of importance, we should usually be very quiet. We are expected to move quietly and speak with a well-modulated voice. There is no place for idle chatter since we must give our full attention to the important person we are with.

Unfortunately there is very little of this type of respect shown today. Society has become so industrialized and Christians have succumbed so much to its pressures that both their personal and family lives are void of silence. Instead, they are impatiently running from one task to another, all the time trying to make their children fit into their schedules. They even relax in a hurry. And as the pressures increase the voices get louder and more strained and the child just becomes another item on the schedule—an item which demands time which they can't afford. As a result we're becoming known as a generation of "screaming" mothers and "angry" fathers.

That brings us to the letter *P. P* stands for "patience." Scripture says, "In your patience possess ye your souls" (Luke 21:19, KJV). This principle applies to our children as well. If we truly love our children and desire to "possess" their souls for the Kingdom of God, we will seek the Lord with all our might until His Spirit works the patience of Christ into every facet of our personality.

Let the second *E* of respect stand for "earnestness." We are in earnest in our service to people whom we respect. Nothing will be allowed to stand in the way of our becoming all that the children need in Christian parents.

Let the *C* in respect stand for "carefulness." A careful person does not overlook the small details of another person's needs. The service of a careful person is complete because the person serving is not neglectful of the inherent value of the person served in each aspect of their relationship.

And finally, let the *T* of respect stand for "transparency." A transparent person is easily understood. He never pretends to be someone he isn't. Instead, he is open and approachable. He is not afraid to tell others what God is doing in His life.

Judges 2:10 tells us why children often fail to follow the Lord. "And all that generation also were gathered to their fathers [died]; and there arose another generation after them who did not know the Lord or the work which he had done for Israel." The following generation did not know the Lord because when they were young children their parents failed to explain to them what God was doing for them personally. They failed to openly confess before their children their utter dependence upon the Lord in everyday circumstances. In short, they lacked "transparency" with their own children.

These seven aspects of respect—recognition, expression, silence, patience, earnestness, carefulness and transparency—speak to us of further commitment to Him who directs our "journey" until "when he appears we shall be like him." For His respect does not waver as we grow and develop but watches and waits to see new ways in which to serve us. According to Him we are always worthy of attention, service, love, care, and consideration.

And because He feels this way about us, He also insists that we embrace this same attitude toward "the least of his brethren." His righteous judgments are based upon this very issue.

"Verily I say unto you, Inasmuch as ye have done it unto one of the least of these my brethren, ye have done it unto me" (Matt. 25:40, KJV).

5. *Examine Your Eye*

The Chinese language uses two words to define "crisis": danger and opportunity. When we consider the awesome responsibility of training children in today's society, we can easily be overwhelmed by the grave dangers that exist. However, the opportunities in working with children are never built upon fear but rather upon a positive attitude and approach toward the child and his circumstances.

Matthew 6:22 says, "The eye is the lamp of the body. So, if your eye is sound, your whole body will be full of light; but if your eye is not sound, your whole body will be full of darkness. If then the light in you is darkness, how great is the darkness!"

If our attitude or perception of life is always negative, fearful or restrictive, it will be very difficult for us to actually see our child's circumstances as opportunities for personal growth and development, both physically and spiritually, and eventually we ourselves will become a hindrance to the child. Instead, we need to realize that God is at work in even the smallest of details, and we need to cooperate with Him by putting into the small child's life experiences and relationships which will build him up for an entire lifetime.

For example, small children need opportunities to become properly independent—independent from hindrances and afflictions that thwart the performance of worthwhile work. This means independence from things such as our "too quick to help" interference when he attempts to carry a big box or to climb a steep stairway.

What a child needs to do is best done alone, by himself,

without a helping hand or an intruding commentary such as, "My, what a big boy [or girl] you are!" How tiring we ourselves find it when we have to "play to the galleries," while at the same time under the pressure of very demanding work. The work itself requires all our attention. And the distraction of an audience, even a most approving and interested audience, drains our energies.

This is also true for the small child. He deserves to be left alone when he needs to be exercising his muscles, to be developing his sensitivities, and to be making his choices. Of course, we do not leave him alone in an unsafe environment to make choices beyond his capability and beyond the safety he needs. But surely we can leave him free to climb a stairway, for example.

He begins as a crawler. Do we need to concern ourselves if he chooses to crawl up or to crawl down, headfirst perhaps? If the atmosphere around him is calm and peaceful, if no sudden noises are made, he will be able to concentrate well on the difficult task and slowly go up and down without a tumble. If the child panics, we are there to help him. We turn him around to a position that makes the climb easier. We can even put his knee here, his hand there for him. A little help when needed instills security. However, if because of fear on our part we forbid the child to climb or to experiment with his world, we build into him that same fear and hesitancy which we experience. Instead, we need to encourage him to solve problems himself. Each problem solved will encourage him to expand his knowledge and ability.

Perhaps he may next try the stairs standing up. He may cling to the railing at the side. Or he may put his hands on the next step and try to step up that way.

Walking down may be even more interesting. Often his legs are scarcely long enough to make the step. And the view! How different the familiar space down below looks from the height of several steps up! It is worth the effort to climb up and down to see everything so familiar and yet so changed.

But what if we decide to interfere? What if we continually whisk him up in our arms, feeling the cuddly body close to ours, feeling big and strong as we help him up those long, hard stairs? Or, worse yet, what if we lack trust in his body's abilities to negotiate the stairs and fear a fall or a bump every time we see him approach the stairs to do his own work, the work of learning to climb? What "kind" and "generous" and presumptuous hindrances we become to the young one trying to become a walker and a climber! We have traded his independence, his coordination, his equilibrium for our temporary sensations of bigness, warmth, and saviourhood. He needs his exercise. We do not need to have our bigness and our strongness reinforced all the time.

All these details are worth thinking about. After all, our lives are not made up of a series of large decisions. Rather, we are what we are because of the string of small, very small, minute-by-minute decisions we make.

Sometimes it is very, very difficult to catch hold of ourselves and take a really good look at what we unthinkingly are doing. But this is necessary if we are to be good to the children God has entrusted to us.

I remember the big tree in the backyard of the children's school when they were five and seven. At that time I had the responsibility of watching all the children during their lunch playtime. I liked the responsibility very much because I was able to observe all the children. There were thirty-five or so of them; their ages ranged from two years old to nine. They were fascinating to watch.

The big tree provided "work" for the school children. This didn't come to my attention, however, until one of the mothers complained. She kept seeing children high up in the tree, in the topmost branches in fact, as she drove up to the school at the end of the school day. Most of the parents had already come for their children, and the remaining ones played in the backyard while the teachers cleaned up the rooms.

One of us was in the yard with them, of course, but we were used to their climbing and gave no thought to it. The anxious mother wanted the tree made off-limits for all the children, or at least for her son who was six.

I went out into the front yard and looked back at the treetop which was visible above the roofline of the school. It *was* very high. I could see that it might frighten an adult to see the head of a child here or an arm of a child there in those high, swaying branches. I had not realized how we looked from the outside.

I went home and gave the matter some hard thought. The mother was a good friend of mine, and I knew we could discuss the subject. But what was at stake? The more I thought about the tree and the climbing children, the more I sensed that the issue was something important. At last I verbalized it to myself: Only those children who *could* climb *did* climb the tree. The climbing was based on their physical development. When they had the coordination and skill to do so, they did so. They never seemed to try to climb further or higher than they felt comfortable in doing. They were not yet into a stage of taunting each other to do bigger or more demanding things. Each did what he was able to do, as far as he was able to do it. Because this general expectation was the basis for all their work indoors, it was a natural transition for them to apply it to the tree.

In the beginning of the school year, we had laid down some rules with regard to the tree. No one could hurt it. This meant no leaf-pulling, no branch-breaking. Following upon this rule, it was easy to tell them that two of them could not climb on the same branch "because then you're too heavy for the tree and will break it." This eliminated the possibility of two or more of them getting on the same branch, trying to get past each other or trying out dangerous stunts. The rule protected them and the tree and had eliminated problems at the beginning.

One other rule helped too. Nobody could boost another person into the tree. This meant that the adults supervising the play yard would not be continually besieged with plaintive pleas to "put me up in the tree, please."And the children were forbidden by this rule to help boost each other into the tree. When a child had gotten up into the tree, he was obviously *able* to do so; he had attained the measure of strength and coordination necessary to do so. Also, no one helped him get down. He had to get himself back down. This added rule further saved us from bumps and bruises and contentions. Someone might climb up repeatedly and expect his fellows or a long-suffering adult to get him down from the last low limb. But if he knew he would have to get himself down after he had gotten himself up, he would think twice about whether he really felt like making all that effort to climb the tree. It was work!

It was scary enough out on the limbs to prevent them from crawling farther out than was safe. And they were light enough to be safe at heights and on small limbs.

This climbing had gone on for a long time, for months, in fact, so I tried to balance the mother's request against the values the tree-climbing had for all the children. I was sure that many, if not most, of the adults would be feeling as she did if they saw the children in the tree.

I went back to my friend.

"I think I know how you feel," I said. "I hadn't known how scary all that tree-climbing must look from the street." (There were no houses around so no neighbors had been worrying about the same tree-climbing.)

"But the climbing is really valuable to the children." I told her about the rules we had laid down at the beginning. And I told her of our safety record: no spills or even close-calls all year.

"I believe you," she said. "But I just can't take it. I get terrified everytime I see them up in the tree."

We compromised. I promised to watch them even more carefully. And she promised never to raise her eyes above the roofline of the schoolhouse as she drove up in the afternoons. We figured that what she did not see would not scare her, even if she knew that nothing was changed.

There was the matter also of their wanting to climb other trees, at home or elsewhere. We made it clear to them that rules at school might not apply elsewhere. Every place they went, there might be different rules. If the adults somewhere else did not want any tree-climbing, then there was no tree-climbing. They had already learned that they had to live in two worlds when they came to school. The adults at school expected different things from them than the adults at home. This was no problem to the children. They adjusted quickly. Differences with regard to tree-climbing was simply one more adjustment they had to make.

But my friend's son soon wanted to climb their tree at home. She, in the meantime, had been giving the subject much thought. She became convinced of the value tree-climbing was having for him in his equilibrium, coordination and balance. (He had had a difficult birth and his equilibrium and coordination had been somewhat affected by this.) She was willing, with her head, to let him climb the tree at home. But still she had to contend with her emotions. She was as frightened as ever about his climbing.

We talked it over. It seemed that the problem was hers, not his. What she had to do was to take steps to keep her problem from becoming his—that is, she had to keep her fright from infecting his confidence in his tree-climbing ability.

"Maybe you could just breathe slower and deeper." This sounds silly, but I have found that it is hard to breathe slowly and deeply and still experience terror. If I could not control terror, I *could* control my body by means of my breathing. And when I controlled my body to this small extent, I found that my emotions began to get under control also.

She worked out the situation very well with her boy. She told him quite frankly how frightened she was when he was tree-climbing and how much she wanted not to be. He promised not to climb very high at home—"just a little climb," he said. She promised to keep her distance and not scare him by her fright. It worked out well. He climbed a little at home, acceptable to him because he could climb all he needed to at school. And she got over a little of her fright—not much of it, but a little. The tree had given them both the opportunity to grow.

We had only one child to abuse the privilege of tree-climbing and to use it to defy an adult. This was a new child who came some time after the opening of the school year. He was six or so, wiry and strong. Up he went one day, shortly after he had joined the school, right at the end of the play period when he knew that all of us would be soon going inside.

"Come on down," I said. "You know we're going inside now."

"You can't make me," came the reply.

With that, I tucked my long skirt into my belt, swung myself into the lowest branch, reached up to him, tucked him under one arm and swung myself down. That reply had made my adrenalin flow! No child was going to put himself out of the reach of authority in *that* backyard.

(Actually, I had been prepared to do just this all along if the occasion ever arose. When I was making clothes for school that year, I made my skirts floor-length—this was in the mini-skirt era—so I could sit on the floor comfortably with the children, so I could chase them if I needed to, and so I could tuck up my skirts and climb the tree if one of them got up and would not come down.)

Without a word, I carried him through the back door. I put him down in front of me and looked him in the eye:

"When you act like a small child, I have to pick you up and carry you like a small child." I did not say anything else. I went on with my work. He went on with his. He was very respectful to me thereafter.

The children who had observed through the window the historic climb I had made were very impressed with my strength. "She carried him under her arm just like anything!" they whispered. Thank God for adrenalin! The children felt very secure in the backyard with a grown-up who could climb up the tree and bring someone down under her arm like a sack of potatoes. (I enjoyed my increased prestige.)

But the most exciting part of the tree-climbing came when I saw a marked difference in the concentration and intellectual ability of one of the children immediately after he had learned to climb the tree. He had always been generally scattered in his ability to concentrate. He would move around, do a little of this, a little of that, but he did nothing long enough to learn to do it well.

He had hung around the base of the tree from time to time, never making an attempt to reach up and try to climb up to the lowest limb. He would watch the other children climb. But he was not ready to take on the tree.

Then one day he climbed the tree. I was there. I saw the climb from start to finish. He jumped up. He grabbed the tree with both arms. He struggled painfully, inch by inch, till he could grasp the lowest limb. It was about five and a half feet from the ground. He hung there, suspended, legs around the tree trunk, hands holding the limb. I watched, out of the corner of my eye. Only a couple of children were in the tree, in branches high, high above. No other children were near the base of the tree; he had the lower part of the tree to himself.

He rested a moment, sloth-fashion. Then he began to struggle, changing his hand hold, "scrooching" his knees up the tree trunk. Somehow he managed to get upright on the first limb. Then up to the next limb he went. Up one more. Up another. He sat there awhile. Coming down was easier. He seemed more confident. At last he was on the ground again. I gave a small explosion of breath. He had done it!

It was time to go inside. He went in, straight to some mathematics material. He sat down. He worked with the material the rest of the afternoon, almost two hours. What intense concentration! It was a transformation. He was a different child.

The transformation was a real one. His concentration continued day after day, though not in such an unusual two-hour stint. That had been like a dam bursting, a dam holding back intellectual energies. His whole personality seemed to change radically from that day forward.

It was as if the coordination of his large muscles had either been parallel with some coordination within his thinking powers or had actually released those powers.

We may never know what part a pot or a pan or a heavy block of wood or an empty cardboard box or a tree may have in the development of our children. We need to give them the opportunity to explore, to move things, to carry things, to get inside things, to get on top of things, to put things into other things, to bang on things, to squeeze through things, to climb up on things, to roll inside things.

Children also need the opportunity to get their own hurts and solve their own problems.

We allowed Paula to go into an older class the year she attended the school with the backyard tree. She was only five but was ready for the work in the six-to-nine-year-old room. This made for a social problem for her, though. The only other girls in the class of twelve children were three girls aged seven. Seven is very much older than five. At least the seven-year-old thinks so.

There are all sorts of little girls too. Some are quiet, some are shy, some are boisterous. These were catty. All three of them were. The odds of having three catty little seven-year-old girls in one class of twelve children seems pretty remote. But there they were!

Paula suffered all spring. What could I do? You cannot control children's social behavior. The three snapped and snarled at each other, continually making each other miserable, as if their only desire in life was to reduce each other, and Paula, to tears.

It would have helped if the older children's playtime had coincided with the younger children's playtime. Then Paula could have played with the younger ones. But this did not always happen. Often she was entrapped with the three older girls on the playground as well as in the classroom. What a woeful situation!

"It's just not fair, Mama," she would cry to me. It was true. She was too old for one group, too young for the other. A kind-hearted older girl, or even a girl who tolerated her, would have been heaven-sent for her. Best of all would have been a girl close to her own age and interests. There was not much I could do. Grown-ups can modify children's behavior with regard to the worst actions. But the little sly afflictions are impossible to catch, and even if caught, difficult to punish. Protection for the wounded child is a poor second best. He needs to be with the other children. He suffers from the isolation. The others go on their way, unfeeling, unsuffering.

Wounds can take a long time to heal. They may affect us in ways we do not realize. When she was ten, Paula had a several-month bout with a friend. There was contention, contention, contention between them in their schoolroom. Both seemed at fault. Envy was proceeding from one side. Inconsiderate behavior proceeded from the other.

Their teacher began to pray about the girls. She saw clearly that Paula needed a good friend her own age. The teacher did not know of the previous sad half year Paula had had when she was five. But the teacher saw, as she prayed, that Paula needed a best friend, a bosom friend, one her own age. The little girl with whom she had been contending was the only girl her age in the school, the only possible candidate for that best friend. And here they were, acting like vixens.

I was desperate. If keeping Paula out of school for a few days would help things settle down, I was ready to try that. But the teacher said that that would be too extreme, that prayer and time and talking with the girls would help.

In the meantime the teacher began to pray for Paula to have a best friend, one that she could truly love and trust. Later in the school year the best friend arrived: from New Zealand. Oh, what love the two girls had for one another! It was a beautiful relationship. And the relationship with the other girl had been healed. The fussing had stopped. They had both come to a good understanding about the other's needs. And they had made some rules for themselves to keep themselves in line at their most vulnerable times during the school day, with ample notes to themselves and with special help and encouragement from the teacher.

But then the best friend went with her parents out of the country. Paula was heartbroken. I asked the teacher, "If it hurts so much, was it worth having such a friendship?" She replied, "Of course it was. Every friendship is worth all we can give it." I was doubtful. I had to live with the pain. It was silent pain. But it was pain. She had found her friend after all these years. And she had lost her.

But good surprises conclude this story. Paula made a trip to a conference with her father a year later. There at the conference was her friend! What times they had! They worked together, played together, confided and dreamed, to their heart's content. She came home very happy. The conference had been good because they had needed her to do many helpful things and because her friend had been there and they had been able to do them together. She was content. She did not miss her friend anymore. The void had been filled with the renewed friendship at an older level. It became less intense, less wishful. It was part of her life, but a more remote part now.

And the best surprise was the beautifully developing friendship with her old partner in contention. The girls were older now, and though older does not necessarily mean better, it did for them. It is as if a generous sponge had sponged out of them the memories of all their old ways and hurts.

Opportunities are not always what they seem to be. They may appear as faults in other people, lacks they have which affect us in vital areas. This could be an opportunity to force us to grow in a certain area.

Opportunities that help us see the children as they are come in perhaps unexpected ways. The big tree in the school backyard showed me some things about the children's development and their need to use their muscles and the possible relation between muscular coordination and thinking and concentration. Then come the painful opportunities, usually called problems. The children get hurt inside, and they learn from the hurts, just as we do.

We may need to see better the opportunities we have. A backyard tree, a quarrel at school could be opportunities for them, and for us, to grow.

6. Choosing Their Heritage

Fortunate is the child who can say with the Psalmist David, "The lines have fallen for me in pleasant places; yea, I have a goodly heritage" (Ps. 16:6). And happy will be the parents who along with the Apostle Paul can say in all honesty, "Now you have observed my teaching, my conduct, my aim in life, my faith, my patience, my love, my steadfastness . . . continue in what you have learned" (2 Tim. 3:10, 14).

Paul had given his spiritual child, Timothy, a heritage. He not only spoke the truth of the gospel but he also lived and worked with Timothy openly and consistently, demonstrating what he believed by the life he lived. As a result Paul was never disappointed in Timothy. Timothy received a "goodly heritage" from his spiritual father as well as his physical mother and grandmother and became a real joy to them, a truly spiritual and faithful young man.

Most Christian parents have the same desire for their children—spiritual maturity and faithfulness. Perhaps they have even made the same request that Paul prayed for the Colossians, "asking that [their children] may be filled with all spiritual wisdom and understanding to lead a life worthy of the Lord, fully pleasing to him, bearing fruit in every good work and increasing in the knowledge of God" (Col. 1:9-10).

Sometimes, however, we fail to see the part that we have in the answer to this request. According to Webster, a heritage is "the rights, burdens, and status resulting from being born in a certain time or place." It also implies "something

handed down from one's ancestors or the past, as a characteristic, a culture, or a tradition." Although we as children
could do nothing about the heritages we ourselves received,
now as adults God is giving us the privilege of making
choices. We not only can stop any worthless heritages from
being passed on to our children, but we can also choose
what our children's "goodly heritage" will be. We can ac-
quire new views and attitudes that correspond with God's
desires for our children and for ourselves.

Let me tell you about some of the heritages my husband
and I decided to build into our children's lives. Psalm
119:147-148 says, "I rise before dawn and cry for help; I
hope in thy words. My eyes are awake before the watches of
the night, that I may meditate upon thy promise."

When Eric and Paula were small, they would climb out
of their beds early each morning and come to me on the
green sofa. I would be praying out loud but quietly. One
would lie down on one side of me and the other on the other
side of me, both of their heads in my lap. I would continue
praying just as I had been, without changing the subject or
my vocabulary. They would just lie there listening for half
an hour or more. Then they would get up and go back to
their bedrooms to dress.

This was the beginning of a heritage of daily prayer and
praise. It wasn't necessary for me to tell them they should
pray. They needed no lectures on the importance and value
of prayer or the joy of praise. Instead they observed my conduct. They saw that I was steadfast through my daily rou-
tine. They also began to perceive what was really important
to me because it was the first thing I did each morning. And
because I was experiencing joy and peace before their eyes
through prayer and praise, it was an experience they desired to have also.

Besides this, prayer was the heritage which taught them
how to establish priorities. Psalm 5:3 says, "O Lord, thou
dost hear my voice; in the morning I prepare a sacrifice for

thee and *watch.*" In other words, through early morning prayer the Psalmist was ordering or planning his day and establishing his priorities according to God's plan for him.

Eric and Paula are also accustomed to asking God what He wants them to do. Besides their early morning time of prayer, from the time that they were six and eight years old, we would get down on our knees with the children a few times every year and pray, "Lord, what are the things You want Eric and Paula to be doing? And what are the priorities among these things?"

The answer to these questions was always an intriguing process because God would bring things up which we would never have thought about. I remember the time when we asked the Lord what Eric should be doing during his summer break. Among some very usual summer activities, the Lord indicated that Eric should study Chinese. Eric was eleven at the time. We knew no Chinese people anywhere in our city. But we said, "All right, Lord," and went about our business with our "antennae" stretched out to pick up any further signals.

One day, weeks later, a friend of mine gave me a brochure of the summer school program at the local junior college. She thought that I might be interested in taking one of the courses. As I read through the list of courses offered, I noticed "Beginning Chinese for Children!" I could hardly believe it!

Registration for the course was that very day, but unfortunately I didn't have enough money for the $20 tuition.

Eric thought about it for a while. He had been saving money for his post-high-school education and his savings account had reached almost $100.

Finally he said, "I guess Chinese is part of my education too. Do you think I could draw some money out of my account now?" he asked.

I phoned his father. His answer was yes. So, after drawing out his money, Eric enrolled at the junior college, just in time. Later the course was moved to the instructor's home, which was much closer to us than the junior college was. Besides this the class dwindled to six or eight persons, and Eric received much extra attention and help, both in speaking and writing.

This was one of the more startling answers we received when we asked God, "What's on *Your* mind?"

When Eric at age fifteen was reminiscing about our old process of asking God about priorities, he said to me, "Would you help me figure out my priorities now?"

His feet propped up on the end of the couch, we began. I hardly said a word. He asked the Lord questions, waiting silently for the answers. When they came he would say, "Hmm," and write something down in his notebook. This is what he wrote:

"Time with the Lord
 Time with the family
 School, Church
 Band
 Keyboard (piano, organ)
 Running (track)
 French
 Reading
 Other extra-curricular school activities"

The anticipation of receiving a personalized answer to our requests and specific guidance for our daily activities is one of the most important aspects of the "prayer heritage." If we give our children only the *habit* of prayer without helping them to develop the *relationship* of prayer, we are failing to prepare them for the future. Children need to know who they are and to Whom they belong. Only when God, their Father, is brought out of the abstract and made known to them as one who gives them practical everyday instructions and encouragement will their trust in Him mature.

Another "goodly heritage" which we have tried to pass

on to our children is music. According to Scripture the capacity within each person to rejoice and exalt in the presence and character of God is uniquely tied to music.

We sing together a great deal as a family. When Eric and Paula were very small, we sang, "The world is very, very big and I am very, very small. But because God knows my name, I am not afraid at all." Then we graduated to the vocabulary of "A Mighty Fortress Is Our God," all its verses, and many other hymns from different centuries and from various countries.

Treasures upon treasures of Christian experience can be made part of our children's heritage through song. Christian leaders, from the Wesleys' time to those responsible for the current Catholic revival of song, have been keenly sensitive to music's power to motivate Christians to live for God and to witness openly about His character through hearty singing. Children deserve strong words of praise set to good music.

And singing certainly gives pleasure to children. We can take potential problem times and turn them into wonderful experiences together through music.

When the children were very young we made many long trips across town, to and from school each day. Potentially this could have become wasted time. I thought it would be good if we could spend all of our travel time focusing on God.

I called the idea that came to me, "singing the high praises of God." I cut up some nice dark yellow heavy paper into squares. On each square I printed out the words that angels or saints sang to the Lord in the book of Revelation. There were fifteen sets of words. Some said, "Worthy art Thou" in various ways. Some said "Hallelujah!" Other songs said other things. I made three sets of the yellow papers—one for Paula, one for Eric, and one for myself. These were kept in the car at all times. Then whenever we were in the car for any length of time, we would take out our papers and sing these praises together. Each person would make up his own tune.We gradually developed a spontaneous expression of praise to God and a freedom and lack of embarrassment with each other. Truly our "noise" to the Lord was "joyful."

Singing the words of Revelation helped the children enter into the heritage of Abraham, Isaac, Jacob, Joseph, Reuben, Benjamin, Judah, David and many other saints of God who have sought to pass on what was theirs.

Singing to God has always been important for God's people. Psalm 68:32 says, "Sing to God, O kingdoms of the earth; sing praises to the Lord." God's eternal purpose and goal for all nations involves praising God through song. But it can only be accomplished through individuals as they begin to follow God's Word literally, and structure their lives and the lives of their children accordingly.

Psalm 68:24-27 says, "Thy solemn processions are seen, O God, the processions of my God, my King, into the sanctuary—the singers in front, the minstrels last, between them maidens playing timbrels: 'Bless God in the great congregation, the Lord, O you who are of Israel's fountain!' There is Benjamin, the least of them, in the lead, the princes of Judah in their throng, the princes of Zebulun, the princes of Naphtali."

The Lord reminded me that I, as a Christian, was truly one of those "who are of Israel's fountain." My spiritual heritage is from him and I need to rejoice in it, enjoying its benefits now as well as recognizing that it is part of my future, and part of my children's future.

Actually the future is what "heritage" is all about. All that we pass on to our children, every choice that we make concerning their lives, should ultimately have their earthly as well as their eternal future in mind. I thought much about this when my children were young. I wanted them to be world citizens. I wanted them to feel a loyalty to many nations at a real and deep level, and I wanted them to feel at home both emotionally and culturally anywhere in the world.

It was the first half of the sixties when they were born, and we were living in a southern city. A white suburban neighborhood was home for us. I wondered what I could do to provide our children with the opportunity to have friends from a variety of economic and racial groups. How were they ever going to have any black friends while they were growing up? Any poor kids as companions? You had to drive for miles before reaching the nearest black section of town. The parts of town that were not middle class were miles away as well. Besides this, at that time bus service did not connect either the black community or the poor neighborhoods with our neighborhood.

However, the women's society of the church we had joined set aside one Tuesday a month for local outreach projects. The fall Eric was born—in fact, days after his birth—I went to the annual opening tea of the women's society. At this time each year an array of studies and projects were presented for the women's consideration. One of the monthly outreach projects was the formation of a team of women who would go to the poorest section of the county, across town, into an all-black community, to work with the children kept by a black pastor and his wife in their church. I was immediately interested.

My first visit to that black church, named Tabernacle, completely captured me. I wanted to stay when it was time to go home. There was so much work to be done and so few people to do it! When I faced the situation realistically, however, the Lord showed me that I was supposed to teach music to the Tabernacle children. So each week I picked up some rhythm instruments from our church, drove to the black church, and taught simple songs and rhythms to groups of twenty children, an hour for each group throughout the day, until everyone had had a music class. There must have been a hundred and thirty or forty children at

that time. During the summer I did other things there together with the college fellowship from our church—for example, tutoring black teenagers in their school subjects.

In all of this Eric always went along, in his pouch at first
and then hand in hand. They nearly rubbed his skin raw
some days. Some of these children had never been near a
white child before, and his color and hair texture fascinated
them. They stroked him and stroked him wherever his skin
showed and he thrived on it. I do not remember his ever crying there. Somebody always had him freshly diapered and
his hair smoothed down at any moment of the day you
might choose to examine him. If any baby ever got constant
attention, conversation and stroking, he did.

During Paula's first year, though, the regular trips to
the black community had to stop. Actually, eight years
elapsed before I was able to work with them on a regular
basis again. In the meantime, however, we did "second
best." Sometimes I would "borrow" two or three children
from the black neighborhood to stay for a week or so with
us. The pastor's wife would arrange it for me. I think she
would tell the folks that "a rich white lady wants to keep
your boy [or girl] for a week." With whatever type of expectations she and they might have had, I was hoping only for
continued contact with black children, not only for the
benefit I could give them, but also for the much greater
benefit their acquaintance provided for my children.

It wasn't until several years later that I noticed how
valuable these relationships actually were. One day when
Eric was in the fourth grade he came home from school and
told me, "Do you know what?" He was bubbling over with
amazement. "Nobody in my class has any black friends."
He paused to let that "unbelievable" announcement hit
me. I let it hit me.

"Really?"

"Really!" He munched on his after-school apple a moment or two, considering the revelation he planned to give

me next. "And some of the kids haven't even ever *seen* any black kids. Or grown-ups either."

"My, my," I said. "That's something, isn't it?"

"Yep. I feel so sorry for them. They don't know anything. So I told them about my Tabernacle friends and about all the stuff we used to do. And they really wanted to hear about everything and they felt kind of lonesome. You know?"

"It's kind of sad, isn't it?" I ventured.

"It sure is," he said, feeling sad for all his culturally deprived suburban classmates.

"Well, you see, it's hard to get to make black friends when they don't live anywhere close by, so I had to make some special efforts to go across town in those days so you could have friends and so you could feel like you feel today—as if they are your friends even if you don't see them as much anymore."

"You make good choices, Mama. You think up good things to do."

I was near tears after such appreciation. The choices we had made were not always easy, but we knew that they were correct because they lined up with God's purposes for every Christian. Matthew 28:19 says, "Go . . . and make disciples of *all nations.*" How could we ever justify ourselves before God and our children if we passed on only the benefits of the gospel to them without also preparing them for the responsibilities inherent in the gospel? This responsibility involves "being all things to all men" (reaching out to all peoples in all cultures).

With such concerns in the family's thinking it didn't take us long to make up our minds when later the Holy Spirit directed us toward becoming part of a missions-oriented Christian community. It was in this environment that the children were exposed to a still broader cultural base. On the mission base their French teacher was a young lady from Scotland. Their science teacher had been born in

Colombia, and their English teacher in Burma! And our pastor was an American-born Japanese.

One year, while we lived in another country, the children went to school and did all their school work in that country's language. The perspective of world history they received in that language, in that setting, has deepened their understanding and compassion for the many people still waiting to experience the love and truth that will set them free from sin. And the additional insights into the various cultures enable them to truly be peacemakers.

Another heritage that children deserve is the privilege of sharing and working with us adults. Not only do they need work to do, but they also need parents who demonstrate to them that work is a blessing.

So many people have read what God spoke to Adam after Adam sinned (Gen. 3:17-19) and have drawn the conclusion that work is a curse. However, they fail to remember that God worked in creation and is still working. Work is meant to be a blessing, a creative opportunity for us to enter into godly purposes and the expression of His nature. Work gives dignity to our existence.

As Eric and Paula grew in their ability to work, I encouraged them to work with me in ministering to others. They helped me prepare environments for groups of small children at the Tabernacle church's day-care school.

In the room for two-year-olds we put a fish tank with a tiny rocking chair next to it so that small observers could rock while watching the fishes' fascinating movements. We also put four or five little, but hardy, potted plants on various shelves about the room. On one of the shelves we kept a small round green tray with a yellow and green pitcher. A tiny square of cloth lay beside the pitcher. The little pitcher contained just enough water to water all the plants for one day. That way any of the children could water all the plants during the day without over-watering them. The child with the pitcher would carry the tiny cloth along as he made his rounds from plant to plant, catching the final drip with the cloth after each watering. Then when the child had finished, the pitcher and cloth were returned to their places on the round green tray.

This one piece of work included decision-making, initiative, discipline and order, and the satisfaction of completion—all aspects of God's work in creation and qualities which He wants to develop in the children as well as in us. In the same way that our maturity depends upon our ability to work, solve problems, take responsibility and assume stewardship over things and people, so also the spiritual maturing of our children is subject to the growth of these qualities in their lives.

One day I said to Eric, "Look at this side of the room. When I put the new curtain there, the balance doesn't seem right anymore." I wanted to encourage his ability to solve problems, so I left him standing there and went off to vacuum the rest of the house.

I wondered what he would think of. The curtain on the large window made the room look low and squatty. Before long he called me back to hear his suggestion.

"How about moving this picture from here to there?" he asked. I thought about his suggestion for a few seconds, wondering what else could be done to work along with his suggestion. Moving only the picture would not solve the whole problem, but the initiative behind his idea was something I wanted to encourage and praise, so together we started with his suggestion and finally achieved the complete arrangement *we* wanted. We smiled at each other. *We* had done it. The key word for building a heritage of work and sharing for our children is *we*.

Obviously the children's decisions and evaluations of situations are not always going to be our highest choice, whether artistically or practically. But for the sake of the long-range goals we have for our children, we need to lay aside our ideas of perfection and convenience. For example, all four of us, ages six, eight, thirty-two and thirty-four, needed to be able to find, reach, and use everything in our kitchen. This included silver, china, glasses, pots and pans. How could we do this with our varying heights? I presented the problem to the children.

They analyzed the situation and the needs and then arranged everything by themselves. I wondered whether any other people had their glasses on a shelf under the kitchen range or their china on the two lowest cabinet shelves, next to the floor. It may have seemed strange to others, but all four of us could reach the table-setting materials in our kitchen. And Eric and Paula had gained a new dignity through having their ideas accepted, not only in conversation but also in the practical structuring of our household.

Perhaps the heritage which is the basis for everything else in our lives is the Word of God. Psalm 119:130 says, "The unfolding of thy words gives light; it imparts understanding to the simple."

As parents our goal should be to impart understanding to our children, that is, to help them "grasp or perceive clearly and fully" the purpose and course of action which God desires to demonstrate through them in relation to the circumstances they experience in life. And this comes only through continual exposure to and assimilation of the Word of God and its underlying principles.

Years ago we bought the records of the New Testament from the American Bible Society. These recordings were originally created for the blind, but we wanted to use them for another reason. We realized that the early formation of the mind is directed not only by what a child sees but also by what he hears. Therefore we decided to program basic thinking patterns into our children from the Word of God.

Each night as the children were falling asleep, they listened to John or Matthew or Luke. Eventually they listened to records from the Old Testament too. This continued nightly for eight years. Each night the bedtime conversation would go something like this:

"Want to hear the same record?"

"No. Let's do the flip side of Acts tonight."

Or, "Let's play some Psalms instead."

In this way the plain Word, without comments, without favorite passages, worked itself into the very bone and marrow of the children's personalities. It became the touchstone for all their aesthetic, relational and moral judgments.

When Eric was fourteen he used to practice for track on the neighborhood sidewalks. One day when he was training with an older boy, the older boy thumped Eric into a big cactus plant. Afflicted by the painful cactus barbs, Eric shuffled home. As I attacked the barbs with tweezers and needles, I asked Eric why the other fellow had pushed him into the cactus plant.

"Guess he just felt like doing it," he replied. There was no vengeance in his tone of voice, only concern for the one who had injured him. Eric accepted the hurt and chose not to retaliate because he knew the scriptural principle which says, "Beloved, never avenge yourselves, but leave it to the wrath of God; for it is written, 'Vengeance is mine, I will repay, says the Lord' " (Rom. 12:19). He chose to "overcome evil with good."

This was only one of many experiences which proved to me that early and consistent exposure to the Word of God had formed mental patterns that influenced the children's attitudes toward spiritual concepts. It was not a matter of some grown-up's opinion of what they should or should not do. It was truly a matter of the right standards of God having been laid down within them through the Word of God itself. They knew that God had said certain things and that He meant what He said. They agreed with what their father had told them: "If God wasn't serious and didn't really mean business, He would have given us 'Ten Suggestions' instead of 'Ten *Commandments.*' "

There are many other heritages which we can pass on to our children, but in my opinion, none so important as these four:

1. The daily relationship of prayer.
2. The scriptural concept of song.
3. The opportunity of working and sharing in preparation to reach all nations with the gospel.
4. The Word of God and its principles.

The preparation of a "goodly heritage" is our responsibility as parents. Listen to this exhortation from Proverbs 27:23-24: "Know well the condition of your flocks, and give attention to your herds; for riches do not last for ever; and does a crown endure to all generations?"

A "goodly heritage" is not passed on automatically. It takes total commitment to the Lord and His purposes in our own lives and concentrated effort in relation to the next generation. "Do not be deceived; God is not mocked, for whatever a man sows, that he will also reap. For he who sows to his own flesh will from the flesh reap corruption; but he who sows to the Spirit will from the Spirit reap eternal life" (Gal. 6:7-8).

7. *The Way He Should Go*

"Even a child makes himself known by his acts, whether what he does is pure and right" (Prov. 20:11).

It was during our time in Hawaii that I saw this principle demonstrated so vividly before my eyes. We were attending a track meeting when racial conflict broke out on the athletic field. Eric, who was twelve, stuck close to his coach. I was standing behind two boys from another school when I overheard one boy ask the other, "Who won the 220?"

"The Christian did," he replied. "You know, that kid over there."

"Oh, yeah?" The other boy turned to look at Eric.

My heart leaped for joy, not because Eric had won the 220 but because God's Word is true and I had just been given further encouragement to continue along the path the Holy Spirit had laid out for us.

Proverbs 22:6 says, "Train up a child in the way he should go, and when he is old he will not depart from it." From the time I first became a parent I realized that this verse was not meant just to be a solace for parents whose children had rebelled and turned away from the Lord, but that the greater emphasis was to be placed upon the *training*—a training which was to continue in changing degrees until the child was old or mature, walking in a strong and complete relationship "the way he should go."

With that in mind, I needed some answers. What was meant by training? And what are the basic areas of training that children need?

Jesus is our example in all things. Luke 2:52 says, "And Jesus increased in wisdom and stature, and in favor with God and man." The verb increase means "to make greater in size, quantity, value and degree." In other words, Jesus was going through a process, a step-by-step, year-by-year addition to or expansion of His personality and human spirit in relationship to three areas: wisdom and moral stature, favor with God, and favor with man. Under the guidance of His earthly parents as well as His heavenly Father, He was being trained for God's purposes.

Our children must also be trained for God's purposes. First Timothy 4:7b-8 says, "Train yourself in godliness, for while bodily training is of some value, godliness is of value in every way, as it holds promise for the *present life* and also for the life to come." This training in godliness is inherent in the Word of God—the written and living Word.

Jesus said, "I am the way, the truth, and the life." Do you need to know *how* to go about training your child? The *way* is found in the Word. Do you need to know *what* to train your child in? Train him in *truth*. The Word is truth. And, finally, are you wondering what that special ingredient is which will bring spiritual reality to the child through the training process? The power is in the Word itself. The Word is *life*.

Let's examine in detail the three areas where children (and adults) need to be trained in godliness. The first area is wisdom and moral stature. Through the centuries of history no person other than Jesus was so noted for his wisdom as was Solomon. Solomon prayed, "Give thy servant therefore an understanding mind to govern thy people, that I may discern between good and evil" (1 Kings 3:9).

The ability to discern between good and evil is basic to all godliness and all of life's circumstances. As the child moves through life he will increasingly be confronted by circumstances which will require him to make a decision, often a very tough one. Therefore we as parents are responsible to see that he has been programmed with the information which will help him to discern, to make wise decisions, and that he has been given the opportunity to develop his decision-making ability in gradual degrees as he grows up.

A child's early experience in decision-making should always be positive, successful. The possibility of negative results arises from allowing the child more freedom than he can handle. In his early years circumstances need to be structured so that whatever his choice may be he will be choosing good.

For example, when Eric and Paula were young my husband encouraged them to make decisions—not between good and evil, but rather between good and good. He began with the area of food. Choices about food are important. We need to make sure that the choices are between two kinds of good food, however. We can offer them a choice between apple juice or orange juice, between two kinds of cheese, between carrot sticks or apple slices. Better yet, when they are a bit older, they can make themselves an array of choices. They can help prepare containers of after-school snacks to head off that late-afternoon tired spell. A jar of carrot sticks on this shelf, a box of raisins on that shelf of the refrigerator, placed there with his own hands, give the young hungry one freedom to find and choose what he needs when he needs it. Decision-making builds initiative and responsibility.

When our children were about two years old, my husband began by asking them, "Do you want your green beans put here? Or do you want your green beans put there?" Their choice was between two locations. He would touch the two opposite sides of the plate with his spoon as he asked.

"There," replied the two-year-old, pointing his finger at the spot he had chosen. And there the green beans went. Later he began to ask them, "Where do you want your green beans on your plate?" Notice that he did not ask, "Do you want any green beans?" We had already made the decision that they were going to eat green beans, and we expected that they would like to eat green beans.

Our strategy was simplicity itself and very strength-building to the decision-making development of the small child. We saved both children from the burden of making a decision which was far beyond their ability to make (whether or not they *needed* the iron and vitamins contained in the green beans), but yet we were strengthening them in choosing good.

Besides teaching the child how to make a good decision by limiting the availability of choices, we also need to make sure that they are continually exposed to the scriptural basis of good and evil. Then, "for those who have their faculties *trained by practice* to distinguish good and evil," their confidence, both in themselves and in the value of choosing good, will grow.

The next step in training the child involves situations where they can make a choice to do good but where failure to make that choice is not necessarily evil.

Bang, one of the eight-year-olds living on the mission base with us, was visiting our room one day. "I won't be at supper tonight," I told her, "so I can't read the next story out loud that I'm supposed to read. Would you read tonight's story for me?"

Bang looked embarrassed. "I don't think I can," she replied. "Why don't you ask Ian?"

"I know Ian would do a good job," I continued, "but I thought you were the one I was supposed to ask. Maybe I made a mistake. Why don't you ask the Lord about it right now?"

I was standing on a stool, cleaning off a top bookshelf while talking to Bang. I looked down. Bang had closed her eyes. Then, seconds later she looked up.

"He says yes." A big smile spread across her face.

In this situation Bang happened to be a child who was

already dependent upon the Lord, a child who expected God to answer her questions. What happens, however, if the child feels the Lord is saying no? Or what about the child who refuses to even consider doing it or praying about it?

Obviously this is not a moral issue and should not be dealt with as such. Instead, the adult should respect the child's decision, all the while leaving the door open for further opportunities. If Bang had refused I might have said something like, "Okay, Bang. If that's what you've decided, we will do it some other time." In this way we are allowing the child time for personal growth, but yet informing him that he can choose to respond positively in this matter in the future.

The third stage of decision-making involves situations where the child must choose between good and evil. And of course this category always includes the possibility of failure, of choosing evil.

Matches are hard to resist when you are an eight-year-old boy—especially when you have the freedom to walk to and from school on your own without a parental hand to cling to. Matches light fires. That is their attraction.

One day we received a telephone call from the school principal. On his way to and from school Eric had been lighting matches in a neighbor's trash can. He and another boy had been doing this. The family had told the school principal so that he could take the responsibility of telling us and working out the situation.

The principal had found it difficult to believe that Eric had been one of the boys. But he fit the description and so he called him in. The principal expected to be wrong about Eric, but he was not. He was surprised and grieved.

It had taken two of them to have the courage to light the fire. They were responsible and confessed the misdeed immediately.

"Why did you do it?" we asked him later at home.

He shrugged his shoulders. He didn't know, nor had he thought about the consequences—about a fire possibly spreading out of control, about charring the wooden fence behind the trash can, or about other damage they might have done.

"Didn't you know it was wrong to do?" we asked. Yes, he had known it was wrong and had done it anyway. He seemed relieved that the truth was out.

Every child will at one time or another be confronted by this or a similar type good or evil situation. And each child will at some time choose to do wrong. The crucial issue lies not so much in making the wrong choice, however, but in the response of the parents and the correction and teaching which follows.

The Bible says that the choice to do evil is sin and sin must be repented of. Repentance is not basically for God's benefit but for ours. Human beings were never meant to live with guilt. And children are especially affected by it. They may not recognize its symptoms or be able to identify its name but it dramatically influences their present relationships and their future development. Guilt, which is a natural result of sin, is a binding and inhibiting power in their lives and must be broken.

Repentance means a "breakthrough." A child must understand that he has been going "his own way" in contrast to God's way. When he understands that he is going the wrong direction, he can then see the need to turn around, retrace his steps and go God's way.

In Eric's case it was not enough for him to merely apologize to the offended neighbor, all the while continuing to stray from the designated to-and-from school route laid out for him by his parents. He had to apologize, ask forgiveness from the adults involved, clean up the mess he had made, and promise to never do anything like that again. Besides this he also had to walk out his repentance. Each day he had to keep going back and forth from school along the designated route without side excursions of any sort.

In order to do all of this successfully, he had to have a breakthrough in his thinking. He had to see, admit, and live with the reality that what he did or did not do always affected other people, that he was responsible to others also in the use of his time. He had to learn that true repentance means fixing up what you have messed up. And on the rare occasions when that is impossible, there is special grace to accept the fact that you have done something beyond mending. Finally he had to learn that it is just as necessary to forgive yourself as it is to accept and give forgiveness.

When a child is brought to understand and accept this type of repentance (and he can) at a young age, we are helping him to walk in a life of inner freedom. Children will become so used to living with an inner sense of cleanness and contentment that their sensitivity to evil will be very keen. Not only will they discern good and evil by their knowledge of the Word and their parents' instructions, but they will also be guarded in their decision-making by peace or a lack of peace.

Although each child at some time chooses evil, we need to be showing them that they can choose good and that the results of their choices will be far reaching, even in others' lives. Let me tell you about Eric's friend, Jay.

Jay initiated our relationship. The way he did it was interesting. After school each day he began doing his homework in our apartment, usually coming home from school with Eric. Jay's mother had told me how much he needed and wanted to have a friend his own age.

One day Eric had "clean the school" duty, so Jay came in alone.

"Hello," I said, from my study corner on the green sofa. He sat down on the sofa with me and we began to talk. The conversation rapidly fell to his control. He obviously had been waiting for an opening to make a little speech.

"I've been watching your family," he said, "and I like

what I see." Startled, I became all attention. What was coming? "I've decided that it would be a good thing if your family would take charge of my family."

Silence. I was digesting this analysis and plea as quickly as I could. Finally I said, "We will do whatever the Lord has for us to do. I'll pray about it. You're asking us to take on a very serious responsibility. I'm not at all sure what you mean for us to do. Tell me about what you have in mind."

"Well, you know, explain to us how to get along and all." Then he began to share about how he and his sister were trying to adjust to a new marriage for their mother and their new stepfather, Wil. Jay grinned, "My sister and I really are pretty mean to Wil."

I took what Jay said to heart and thought about our conversation several days. Finally, while praying, I got a clear word for Jay. I told him about it as soon as he came in after school that day.

"Jay, listen to what the Lord says. You want to make a friend of Eric. What is going to let you have Eric as a real friend is *your taking responsibility to treat Wil the way God wants you to.*"

Jay looked thoughtful. I tried again.

"Eric and his life won't make any sense to you unless you decide to be in right relationship to Wil and to work at your relationship with Wil. Otherwise, you and Eric just won't be able to relate to one another because you'll be on different wavelengths. Eric *respects* his father."

Jay looked down. "I really do make things hard on Wil. He's really tried his best, and I haven't accepted him."

I had been holding my breath and now I gave a little explosion of relief. I had been on target without understanding well their family situation.

"Well, all I know," I continued, "is that when I prayed for your request—you know, about our family helping your family in some way—this is what I heard: that *you* were to take the responsibility to treat Wil right and that Eric then could be your friend because you boys would be living lives that were alike and you could relate to one another."

He sat thinking for a while. "You're right," he said at last. "I'll do it. It won't be easy. I've made a bad start."

"You'll know what to do," I said. "And I'll check on you from time to time." And that was that. We had made an agreement. I would "oversee" from afar while he would do the living "up close" and "treat Wil right," whatever that meant. I did not know what it meant. But evidently God and Jay knew. That was enough to go on.

Weeks passed. Months passed. I shared with Wil and with Jay's mother our previous conversation and our later agreement. I continued to view things from afar.

I could read some signals in Jay. He was happier. He was settling down in school. Best of all, Eric liked him. That was the best barometer reading I could have. Jay must be doing some things right at home. I took him aside and told him just that.

He sighed, wearily and happily, too. He felt good about my commendation. "I have been trying. But it's so hard. I've got so many bad habits to break. You know, ways of thinking about Wil, ways of talking bad about him, ways of ganging up on him with my sister, ways of acting toward him."

"Yes, but they're just habits. You're making new ones. Don't get discouraged."

"I won't. I'll keep trying."

Jay learned some of his cues from quietly observing Eric's responses to his father. Eric was unaware of this; but Jay studied their relationship and practiced what he observed. Jay chose to respond to a grown-up in ways that helped allow that grown-up to become who he needed to be. Jay treated Wil as a son would act toward his father. And Wil became indeed what he longed to be: a father to Jay. Jay had made it happen. He had ministered life and fatherhood to his forty-year-old stepfather.

All of us make a lot of difference to a lot of people by the choices we make. Few choices are truly private. In many small and large ways we minister life or we minister death to people. We cut them down or we build them up. We disable them or we enable them. We bless them or we curse them, all as a result of our decisions.

Besides training a child to discern good and evil, we must also teach him obedience. Through obedience a child gains favor with God. The call to obedience is the call to be like Jesus. Hebrews 5:8 says that "although he was the Son, he learned obedience through what he suffered."

Obedience involves suffering—suffering on the part of the one who gives a command and suffering on the part of the one who responds to the command. The parent gives up time and attention which might have been directed toward his own pursuits in order to give the attention necessary to command a child to do something. The child in turn gives up his right to initiate action and instead responds to the command, at whatever cost might be involved in terms of time, energy, and personal resources. Together both parent and child pay a price.

I find it necessary to say all this because our culture has become so adapted to doing what feels comfortable and easy at the time. As a result the cost of such behavior patterns has become astronomical to our society and to our personal lives. If we realize from the start that training children in obedience is going to cost *us* some suffering as well as them, we will be better prepared to undergo the training in self-discipline which is required. We cannot be capricious or inconsistent in training children. It takes discipline well learned in our own lives in order for us to teach obedience to them. If a mother does not make her bed until afternoon, she cannot teach a child how to keep his room clean. If a father spends all his evening time reading the newspaper or watching television, he cannot teach his children how to be seeking God in prayer. Neither of them will know how to teach because they themselves have not learned. Learners become teachers.

"Let's play the Czerny book through," I told Eric as he turned to some Andre Crouch piano music.

"*Groan!*" His face contorted in mock agony. It would have been easier to let him play what he liked all the time, but it would not have been right. I knew it would lead him into a blind corner with insufficient development and training to allow him to expand and broaden out in ways that would be important to him later on.

I did not like feeling rejected. It would have been much easier to give him a cheery, "You're doing great!" and pass by the issue. But I had to suffer the rejection and insist on obedience—prompt, cheerful, and complete obedience because I had discerned needs beyond those he felt he had.

This type of obedience is related to the character of the one who gives the command. For example, obedience to Satan would be our utter undoing. We need to learn to *disobey* him and his every suggestion promptly, eagerly, and completely. However, when the call originates in the character of God ("Children, obey your parents in the Lord, for this is right"—Eph. 6:1), we need to obey Him cheerfully, promptly, and explicitly. Obedience which is not cheerful, prompt, and complete is not obedience at all.

It is important for parents to understand their place in regard to a child's obedience. God's desire is that parents and children live together in obedience to Him. We are not under one set of rules and children under another. We are all under the same rule and the rule is: the Kingdom, His domain and jurisdiction over us. We both obey the same rules at differing levels of ability because of our varying levels of development; however, the differences between us, in His eyes, are far less than we can imagine. As adults we often like to feel superior to children. We are not! We are on the same level with the children in God's sight. We, however, have the added responsibility of their care and nurture placed upon us.

When a child obeys his parents, the Lord receives this as having been done unto Him. Children's obedience to God is shown by obedience to us. Likewise, every service, comfort, help, little song, hug, or thoughtfulness done to any child by an adult is experienced by the Lord as done unto Him. "Whatever you have done to the least of these my brethren, you have done it to me." In this way we serve Him through our children and they serve Him through us.

Physically, obedience is an achievement. It is not simply an act of the will. We can see this very clearly with little children, and we must understand this thoroughly in order to be just in our conversations with them and our attitudes and actions in dealing with them.

We stood outside, shivering in the brisk autumn air. The group of little children who were with me leaned against the splintered door frame of the old church. I walked away from them about fifteen yards and crouched down.

"Dwayne!" I called quietly, and waited a moment. "Come to me!"

A line of children surged forward. I met them and put them against the doorway again. "I called Dwayne," I told them, and then returned to my distant position.

"Dwayne!" I called again and waited. "Run to me!"

Dwayne flung himself toward me and I caught him in my arms and turned him around to face the others.

"Cathy," I called. "Run to me!" Cathy shambled to me, chin on her chest, thumb in her mouth.

"Cherri, walk to me." Cherri ran. Then her face split with a grin and she turned back to the doorway and began again, walking with big strides. She lost one of her clogs before she got to me.

"Look what she done!" cried Harvey, disturbed by the lone clog on the sidewalk.

"Don't worry about that, Harvey. You skip to me." He started out, but then, looking puzzled, went back.

"Don't know how to skip," he muttered.

"Then—walk to me."

Harvey could not skip. He was tall, well-coordinated and almost three. But he could not skip. Skipping is quite a complex movement for a child to make. It involves an intricate left-right muscle relationship which many children don't master until they are five or six. My command to him had been one that would have been on the frontiers of his abilities as a three-year-old. I gave the command to see what Harvey could do.

I found out later that Harvey had never seen anyone skip. But when I showed him how and held his hand and skipped with him, he was able to learn to skip quickly. Then he taught Cherri and they would skip around, fascinated with themselves, Cherri shedding her clogs and stumbling over them as they circled back, and Dwayne solemnly commenting from the side, "Cherri done lost her clogs again. She gonna fall!"

Even though a child may understand what we mean when we ask him to do something, this does not necessarily mean that he has the coordination or the concentration abilities to fulfill that command. He may never have seen the action done. Or he may never have seen it done at a pace and in a way which he can comprehend. There is no moral deficiency on his part nor any disobedience toward us. Instead we have lacked the good sense to consider him and his abilities. The fault, if there is any reason to use that word at all, is ours.

Some of our commands need to be exploratory, to see what children can do and what they can reason out. For instance, you might tell a small child, "Bring that to me," as you point at a big empty cardboard box. Then you would watch to see how he solves the problem. He might try to pick it up and carry it to you. He might push it. He might get another child or a wagon to help him carry it. He has the ability to solve the problem of how to fulfill the command, but his choice will depend upon his strength, the obstacles that lay between you and him, and the availability of help.

Other factors involved are his ability to hear and understand the command. When a child hears, understands, and begins to move in the direction of the completion of the command, he is in the process called "obedience." We usually think of obedience as a completed act and judge the terminal result. But that is the by-product of obedience, so to speak, its effect. We value that and look for that, but we should be valuing and looking for the process itself. The fact that we have at last received the box from the child is valueless. However, his effort to please us, to give of his time and ability is a gift of himself. So the quicker we relinquish the desire for an end result and learn instead to value and nurture the process of obedience, the more closely we will be aligning ourselves with the real worth of what is going on around us and between us.

In the command the initiative is with the one who gives the command, who makes the call to do something. The ability to do the thing called for is an issue "negotiated," so to speak, between the two persons. Neither of us may know if the person can really do the thing called for. We both find out in the process. We jointly share the responsibility in this middle area. Good sense, comprehension, effort to act, and effort to communicate back and forth are needed by both sides.

But in the matter of timing the initiative switches completely to the one being called. The parent initiates the call to obedience, but the child is in total control of the timing. In fairness to children, we need to give them commands when they can choose to obey immediately. It is thoughtless, rude, even cruel, to give them commands out of our own needs or to suit our convenience without regard for the concentrated effort they may be expending at that time in another direction. "Come here and help me" can be obeyed promptly, cheerfully, and completely if we have taken the time to look at the child. What is he doing and at what state of doing it is he? It is very necessary for children to develop concentration, and we do not want to interrupt them continually through our whims. They can tell from the tone of our voice when we are in a tight spot ourselves and must have them drop everything and run fast to us. But this tone is not needed daily.

Finally, a child must be trained to "gain favor with man." Although Scripture warns us that the "fear of man is a snare" (Prov. 29:25), still there is this aspect of gaining others' approval. Scripture even goes so far as to say, "When a man's *ways* please the Lord, he makes even his *enemies* to be at peace with him" (Prov. 16:7). Obviously our ways, our "characteristic mode of action or behavior," influences how we are accepted by others.

According to Old Testament culture, the childen were often punished for and along with their parents on account of the parents' sin. The story of Achan who stole the gold and the garments which he was forbidden to take in battle, and the story of Hophni and Phinehas, sons of Eli the priest, illustrate this principle. Most of us are thankful this never happens today! Unfortunately, however, it does. Many times children suffer the punishment of rejection from their peer group or receive the disapproval of adults because their parents have never taught them the correct approaches and responses for getting along with others.

Ephesians 4:29 says, "Let no evil talk come out of your mouths, but only such as is good for edifying, *as fits the occasion*, that it may impart grace to those who hear." Speech and conduct which is edifying and "fits the occasion" is called politeness or the art of social graces. These are not aspects of life which are automatically absorbed by children. Instead, children must be trained to be thoughtful toward others, demonstrating this in their speech and conduct.

When Eric was quite small, four or five, I decided to make him a little tea set. I put together a little wooden tray, a sturdy one-cup metal teapot with a scarlet knob on its lid, four bright blue and yellow enameled cups, a tin of tea, and a jar with a tight lid for sugar. We carried that tea set with us many places. Although we didn't use it much as he grew older, still it always sat in a place of state among the things in his room, a monument to the intention of hospitality—an attitude of thoughtfulness which had been trained into Eric over the years.

It began by training him to speak correctly. This included the use of the simple words "please" and "thank you," "hello" and "good-bye," and "excuse me" and "I'm sorry." These are polite words which influence people and situations more than we can imagine and yet they are becoming strangely absent from the vocabulary of both adults and children. They are words which tend to safeguard respect in interpersonal relationships.

Besides *what* was said, we worked on *how* it was said. Proverbs 15:1 says, "A soft answer turneth away wrath, but a harsh word stirs up anger." This implies not only the choice of words in our response, but the tone of our voice. A mellow, well-modulated voice is an asset to any person.

Along with training them to speak politely, we needed to demonstrate to them what real thoughtfulness and hospitality was. That was one reason why I decided to use china and silver at every meal for our family. If the children were truly my younger brother and sister in the Lord, then every meal had the potential of being like a supper with the Lord himself. Why relegate the china and silver only to those occasions when company comes? Daily bread deserved to be served on china and silver.

I also bought linen napkins for our daily use. "They'll be cheaper in the long run," I thought, "especially considering the cost of paper ones. And they certainly are more beautiful." All of this afforded the children a natural setting for learning gracious behavior.

The idea that children can be taught how to serve others in beautiful gracious ways was once again reinforced when we moved to Hawaii. The Hospitality Group on the mission base had heavy responsibilities. One of their assignments was serving us at the special meal we all had together each weekend. "We'll train the children to serve," they decided. And so they did. They showed the children how. Then each week the children carefully carried the serving dishes to the tables (the many tables), took note of any needs such as extra water or refills, and smiled graciously upon us as they made their way back and forth between us and the kitchen.

Children need to learn about giving. They become more like Jesus, just as we do, as they learn to give of themselves. This concept of giving can be demonstrated in the most simple, "everyday" ways.

"We want to ask your permission to have" (and they named two girls in our community) "over for supper next Sunday night on our lanai." Eric and Jay had a nice little balcony off their room which they called their lanai.

I thought for a minute. It seemed all right to me.

"You know we got prizes for being good guys on the school camp-out. Well, we were going to spend that money on food for ourselves but that seemed a bit piggish so we want to buy ice cream . . . "

" . . . and peaches," added Jay.

"To make sundaes with," I finished their sentence.

"Yeah." The two boys grinned.

"But what will you do for *food*?" I underlined the word with my tone of voice.

"Oh, we'll go down and get the regular food. Then we'll share our prize money—the ice cream and stuff we'll buy Saturday for dessert—with the girls. If that's all right with you. But we want to borrow, if we may, your china and silver. And linen. And the big silver pitcher for water."

Their proposal was quite all right with me.

It was to be a very special dinner. Both boys invited both girls, so no partiality was shown. They had not thought about doing it another way. I was glad. Fourteen is a nice age—old enough to plan and execute challenging projects, but childlike enough to carry them off with simplicity and grace.

Just before the meal, Jay's seventeen-year-old sister Brooke knocked on my door.

"Do you have any aprons?" she asked.

"Yes," I replied.

"One that will go with a gold dress?"

"Well, let's look and see what I have." I opened the drawer where the aprons were kept. "What about this one? It's gold. Does it match your dress?"

"Not exactly. The dress is a brassy gold."

"Well, take a look at this one. Or this. What do you need the apron for?"

"I'm serving the food for the boys and their guests," Brooke answered as she pondered her color choices among my four or five old aprons.

What a dinner that was! What fun they had! And all because they remembered "the words of the Lord Jesus, how he said, 'It is more blessed to give than to receive' " (Acts 20:35). Romans 15:2 restates this principle: "Let each of us please his neighbor for his good, to edify him."

Gaining favor with man (the type of favor God desires us to have) will result in our children's lives as we train them to think, speak, and act to please and edify others instead of themselves.

Let's summarize this aspect of training with Proverbs 3:1-4: "My Son, do not forget my teaching, but let your heart keep my commandments; for length of days and years of life and abundant welfare will they give you. Let not loyalty and faithfulness forsake you; bind them about your neck, write them on the tablet of your heart. *So you will find favor and good repute in the sight of God and man.*"

8. *The Lord Will Rule Over You*

When Gideon returned home from defeating the Mid-
ianites, the men of Israel, thinking to honor him for his
courageous service, asked him to rule over them, to be their
king. Gideon's reply was, "I will not rule over you and my
son will not rule over you; *the Lord will rule over you*"
(Judg. 8:23).

Gideon's answer was far from what the Israelites expected. And perhaps my ideas about making rules for children
will be different from your expectations also. In fact, whenever Christian parents have asked me for advice on how to
stop their children's quarreling or shouting or hoarding, I
have been at a loss. The only advice I have ever given is,
"Remember, Jesus is Lord. Keep affirming that He is Lord.
He will show you what to do."

When either a glowing report or a disappointing one
came back to me after such counsel, I would still be at a loss
as to further advice to give. I only knew that Jesus is Lord. I
could tell a parent to let that truth invade his whole situation. I'm sure that this answer seemed feeble and fumbling
to the parents, but whenever a parent did receive this advice and begin to believe it and act accordingly, the power
of God entered into his situation.

We grown-ups often let situations rule us. Or we let customs around us dictate our responses to our children. Worst
of all, we may put forth our own selves as lords over the
children. We need to respect, and act as if we respect, the
Holy Spirit's direct work with them. The Lord can rule us,
and them, by His Holy Spirit. And we need to believe and

act as if the children can do many, many things for themselves. How else can they grow in self-control?

Often it is easy for a grown-up to be drawn into the role of one who settles all disputes between children, the only one who is the final authority in relational questions. It is not necessary, however, to be swallowed up in that sort of quicksand.

When my own children were small, I took a firm stand within myself about this matter. Their relating was their own responsibility, not mine, just as learning to walk, to talk, and to manage their bathroom needs was their responsibility. I could guide them but I could not do their work for them.

I had no theories about how to help children to relate. But I had given myself to Him who is Lord when I was a small child, when He was presented to me as The Way, The Truth, and The Life. He is Truth, and I wanted to speak truth to the children.

Thus the rule I set for myself was: *Speak the truth in all things.*

This meant that I talked to them as if they were intelligent creatures. Baby-talk was unknown in the household.

I used the word "negotiate" frequently with them during the next four years. In fact, *"negotiate"* became our first household rule and a standard word in our two-year-old's vocabulary. The four-year-old might be wanting pears when the two of them were sent off to the produce aisle of the supermarket to choose one kind of fruit for the family for the weekend. The two-year-old, wanting apples, would say over and over, "You got to negotiate. You got to negotiate." And they did. I did not follow the process. It was their business. They were adept at it. They still are. Surprisingly, matters about which negotiations were needed arose less frequently than I expected. The two of them liked each other so much that they each enjoyed going along with the other's desires.

House rule number two was: *Do what you can do as long as you truly know how to do it.*

Following this rule through to its final conclusions was grueling to me. Once I was committed to it, the rule implies that I had to wait an extra forty-five seconds (precious seconds! impossible to wait! I must go on with what I want to do!) for the short brother to close the house door *himself*, as we dashed out to make an appointment. The rule implied that I had to stand aside and to let each of them wipe their own bottoms as thoroughly as they were determined to do after using the toilet. I might need (!) to wipe them so I could hurry them into the bedroom so I could hurry them . . . so I could . . . My need? Or their needs? The conflict between needs sometimes seemed a moment-by-moment experience. Their real need was to *become.* They had to exercise what they could begin to do in order for it to *be.* My needs? Often imaginary, selfish, or just plain unimportant.

Of course very small children will later need to recognize and adjust to the needs of others, to our needs, too. We all do this. Our teacher has needs. Our boss has needs. We adjust to these external needs.

But for the very small child, his needs are physiologically based, and are serious, vital, growth needs. We need to consider the children and let them practice what they need to practice—forking food, drinking from a cup, opening doors, folding up pajamas—as thoroughly as they need to practice these things.

House rule two may sound grand, noble, and wonderfully ideal. But trying to live my commitment to the covenant of living with very small children under the lordship of Christ was a crucifying ordeal. In the Christian community we nobly, scripturally, and with great theological soundness want each brother to grow into that full likeness of Christ, to develop that full ministry to which our God has sovereignly called him. But dear me! How annoyed I can become with the Lord when that involves the necessity of my being pruned down to the ground myself in order for the Lord to bring my brother forth.

Yes, rule number two may sound noble. But I forewarn you. You will continually die to selfishness living under it.

House rule number three was only a logical extension of house rule two: *When you make a mess, clean it up.*

You spill milk. I hand you a rag. No comment. No help. It is your business; you have to do the cleaning-up, now that you are able to do so.

This sounds simple, though the living of it may strain the tall brother more vigorously than he would like to admit. We are absolutely compulsive about fussing, commenting upon, calling attention to and doing a child's work for him. Full liberty from such presumptuousness may take time to achieve. These compulsions seem stubbornly entrenched in our characters and supported and sanctioned on every hand by many people and many things about us. Only the quiet voice of God's Spirit disagrees with such "normal" adult behavior.

We found that this rule, "clean up your messes," extended on to guide us in those times when we hurt one another. We had made a "mess" between us. If I had made it, I had to clean it up by going to the other one, adult or child, saying, "I'm sorry. Please forgive me." What began as a way to enable to child to feel self-respect and to take care of his environment now in God's grace had broadened out to teach us, and him, to ask for forgiveness and to receive forgiveness and to live in an atmosphere of forgiving and being forgiven.

These were the house rules we lived under. The Lord provided a continuing teaching and ever-increasing grace to flow as I walked through my serious attempt to adhere to the rules.

During the middle years, the emphasis changed somewhat. Though the three rules—(1) Negotiate; (2) Do what you can truly do; (3) Clean up your messes—underlaid everything for them, I continued to grow. I began to expect a life of mutuality with them—my receiving from them as well as their receiving from me. I began to follow through on my role as a mother. I began to live and act more in accord with the ways God wanted me to in that role. The children, for their part, had to understand the boundaries we placed upon them, and they had to keep to those boundaries. I taught them to take on as much responsibility for their own needs and for the whole family's needs as they could handle. This meant, for example, that they learned to clean well areas of the house which they had not especially messed up but were common to us all. This was taught as a service they needed to give to the whole family because the whole family needed to have it done. This seemed very important to me as they went through the six-to-ten-year-old period. And I helped them to pray for whatever needed to be prayed for. "Whatever" came to include many, many things, as you have seen.

During their older years now, the eleven-to-sixteen era, Earl and I are listening to what God is saying to them. And we are listening to Him about what He is saying about them. As for them, they are under two rules: Seek God in all things. Enjoy Him in all things.

I will write out the rules in an outline form so you can see them more clearly:

Setting the Rules

    A. The early years: 0-5
        1. For myself
            a. To go to some effort on their behalf; not to take the easiest way to do things. Do unto them as you would be done by them. This included preparing an adequate environment for them.
            b. To talk to them as if they were intelligent people.
        2. For them

    a. Negotiate.
    b. Do what you can do.
    c. Clean up messes.

B. The middle years: 6-10
    1. For myself
        a. To expect a mutual life with them—my receiving from them as well as their receiving from me.
        b. To follow through on my role as God expects me to.
    2. For them
        a. To understand boundaries and keep them.
        b. To take on as much responsibility for their own needs and for the family's needs as they can handle.
        c. To pray for whatever needs to be prayed for.

C. The older years: 11-16
    1. For ourselves
        a. To listen to what God is saying to them.
        b. To listen to what God is saying about them.
    2. For them
        a. To seek God in all things.
        b. To enjoy Him in all things.

The discipline of setting rules for others for whom you have responsibility, together with appropriate consequences for these rules, is a discipline which we have to learn. The reward or appropriate consequence for fulfilled responsibility is a new, sometimes harder, responsibility. If we rule our families well, God can trust us with other riches.

Some of you from legalistic backgrounds will think that this chapter is too sketchy. I challenge you to live after the Spirit and not after the law. I urge you to believe me when I

say to you that discipline of *ourselves*, and true consideration for children shown in preparing their environments, in
feeding them well, in taking note of their bodies' changes, of
listening to them and to Him, will eliminate before they
ever arise many, if not most, of the difficulties between
child and adult. Our sinfulness affects them, hampers
them. We do not need to create systems of rules for them
nearly as much as we need to get serious about God's rule
over us personally. As we keep hearts pure before Him, He
will reveal the specific rules our children need in the situations in which we live, and He will show us how to give the
children these rules, how to guide them in the keeping of
them, and how to enforce them.

I want to further broaden this subject to include rules
for a group of children who were working together in one environment. This occurs frequently in school, but it may oc-
cur elsewhere, as in prayer groups, or even after disasters,
such as with refugee children.

First, make special note of the environment and how
you set it up, what you put into it and who really will do a
major portion of the rule-setting for children. If you have
chairs that are too big for them and of which they constantly are in danger of falling off and which they can not move
about as they need to, you have obviously set up a
caretaker-type situation wherein you and a team of adults
will have to do things for them and will have to keep wiping
their tears as they fall! Things as simple as ridiculously un-
suitable furniture do not seem to catch the attention of
most well-meaning adults.

If you have real work for them to do, real prayer needs
for them to pray for and see the results of, passages of scripture for them to absorb instead of snippets of verses, they
will have confidence in your good sense and will obey you
willingly and keep the rules you find are needed in the
physical setup you have.

Let me tell you about "Little Seeds."

Our Christian community had thirty children to be taken care of in one room for an hour and 15 minutes each Sunday evening. These children were mostly two-year-olds; there were some threes. The situation with them and with their adult leaders had not been good. There were tears. There were spankings. There was general despair and aggravation.

So Earl and I were invited to organize the "Little Seeds" program. After working with this group for several months, we wrote down the principles which guided this program. (The principles are mainly for working with *groups* of children.) My first set of comments produced instant controversy. Here is what provoked the controversy:

1. Let Little Seeds serve one another. Ignore problems. Ignore tears. Ignore spilled material. Often another child will come to meet the need. Don't interrupt by letting them notice you are noticing.

2. Each person has the right to feel however he feels. There is no "You shouldn't feel that way." If the Little Seed feels like crying, that is his business. He is responsible for handling his own feelings. And I have the right to feel however I feel. If I don't want him to sit on me, for example, I say, "I don't want you to sit on me."

3. A Little Seed is responsible for doing everything for himself that he is able to do. If he says, "Put my work away for me," I say, "No."

4. A Little Seed is not responsible for doing something that he cannot do. If another child doesn't come to the rescue after ten or fifteen minutes (such as cleaning up spilled work), I do it as invisibly as possible.

Ignore problems? Horrors! We were supposed to teach the children to take all their problems to Jesus and to pray about hurts and tears, some of the grown-ups said.

The grown-ups did not understand what I meant. They were dealing and living on a psychological level. I was way back where the the two-year-olds are: on the physiological.

I went to the example of the two-year-old trying to carry a big, big, big box and an adult kindly (!) helping him by taking it from him and carrying it for him.

Then I said, "The children will instantly look at the adult when a child has spilled something. The child expects to be fussed at. He expects to be told to be more careful next time. He expects to be the center of negative attention. After all, that's what he has experienced at home with us in the past." It was true. That is how we adults usually met spills and messes.

"Instead, we'll look the other way and see if he can solve his own problem. He can pick up the puzzle he dropped. He can put its pieces back in. He can take it to its place on the shelf when it's back together again. At least he can if we give him undistracted time in which to do it."

"What if they don't do it?"

"They've *been* doing it." The adults were unbelieving. "Look," I continued, "try it out. Keep your hands off them when they have problems. Keep quiet. Don't even look in their direction. They won't expect that. The new ones won't anyway. See what happens."

They were doubtful. They were reluctant. But they went along with my new idea. The individual children cleaned up their individual messes. Often it took them thirty minutes or so to do it. But they were not on a time schedule. They took all the time they needed to fix up what needed to be fixed up.

Crying was another matter.

"It just doesn't seem right to ignore tears." The grown-ups that were new to the situation were careful to let me know that I was not being very loving in rule number one.

And tears were hard to ignore. Sometimes there was a new child who took two or three weeks to settle in and accept his parents' absence. What did we do? Did we let him wail in a corner all alone? Did we cart him around on one hip while we did other things in the room? Did we try to distract him from his grief with some enticing work? Sometimes we did one thing, sometimes another. Different children needed different responses from us.

But still there was no reason to be especially concerned about tears. I told them, "Suppose a child is crying. He won't cry forever. He'll stop and find something that he likes to do that will be more interesting than crying was. It is not good for them for us to pet them and cuddle them and kiss them and comfort them. They don't need that. They need to become accustomed to the community of children and to the different things that we do. Our adult interference by cuddling them and being concerned about tears really delays the process for the child."

So we compromised. The more tender-hearted adults did a little cuddling but moderated their desires to do more. And I gave attention to the upset children instead of ignoring them. You have to do the sensible thing in a situation. These rules were guidelines, after all.

The point of feeling how you feel was made clear to the child whenever one of us simply put into words the feeling. "You're tired." Or, "You're mad because he stepped on your puzzle." "You feel excited because it's your birthday." The verbalization of itself would often quiet them. They liked having words for what was going on inside.

It was a major hurdle for us adults to consider that the child was responsible for handling his own feelings. Probably it was because it had been so hard for most of us to accept that people do not make us mad. We make ourselves mad at people. Others do not come along and drop some sort of emotion into us which we must passively receive and thus for which we have no responsibility. It is the same with the children. Of course they can provoke one another in various ways, and we can provoke them too. But to a large extent they can choose their responses, just as we can, and we can show them that they can.

"If you want to sit under the table all by yourself, you're going to keep on feeling lonesome. If you try a puzzle, you won't feel lonesome."

That is the truth. The two-year-old who is busily resenting the departure of his much loved parents needs to put that into his head and think it over. If he goes on as he is going, he will continue to feel wretched. If he decides to work, he will stop feeling lonesome. It is his choice. One week he makes the choice one way, and takes the consequences: a headachy miserable hour convinced that he is unreasonably deserted by the important persons in his life. The next week he makes the other choice. He sniffles five minutes or so. Then he goes to work. What a greeting his returning parents receive that night! He is babbling incoherently with his joy at his accomplishments. And so he may teeter back and forth, "halting between two opinions," until he settles into the obviously more comfortable sort of behavior. That is, unless we interfere with the process with attention and concern and worried looks and sympathies that are misplaced. He has to do his own work. We cannot do it for him.

He needs to know that we have feelings too. I do not want the children to start climbing into my lap because then all dozen or twenty or thirty of them will want to. They have laps at home that they can sit on. They will crush me if they all come at me at once. I can say, "I don't want you to sit on me." That is the truth. And the child accepts it.

It was beautiful to watch the children help each other. If the adults had sufficient self-control, often another child would be the comforter of the new child and his guide around the room. Both unable to talk, they would manage to explore everything, in their wordless way, together. Or if the adults did not hurry to help pick up pieces of spilled work and the child still wandered away with the spill left behind, another child would stop and put things back together. They liked to make order out of chaos. Putting things away was very interesting to them. We later would

take the child who wandered off and, pointing to the work
in its place on the shelf, say, "So-and-so put your work back
for you." That way the indirect hint was given that it was
his responsibility to get it back himself the next time. And
he also then had the opportunity to feel glad that another
child had helped him. Sometimes they did need to be called
back and asked to put away their work. But they caught on
to the rules of the room quickly. It flowed without much
comment.

The rules that I wrote out for the adults went on as follows:

1. The environment is the Holy Spirit's chief instrument for teaching Little Seeds. Therefore the environment
is of utmost importance for the Servants to maintain in perfect order.

2. All materials should be perfect each Sunday night.
Any missing parts or dirty pieces must be attended to before the environment is set up the next time.

3. All materials in the environment have a purpose and
are treated with great respect by the Servants. When taken
from or replaced on the shelves, they are to be carried as if
one of the Three Kings were taking his gift to his King.

4. In large measure, for the youngest children in particular, the Servants' chief role is to *serve the material* to the
child, as an intelligent waiter serves a dinner. He, the
waiter, learns the patron's needs, and he serves these needs.
The less one observes his existence, the better waiter he is.

The adults took these instructions to heart. It was exciting to them to work in an orderly place with small children.
Children were not loud! They did not run and tear around
all the time! This was news, good news, to the adults.

I continued with the guidelines for the adults in relating
to the children:

5. Little Seeds are insatiable in wanting to use all their
senses. They are perfecting each sense. In their brains they
are creating order from the confused mass of sense impres-

sions they receive constantly.

6. They absorb the environment through every part of their body—sole of foot, skin, as well as ear and eye and hand. They can make ordered discernment of their impressions if the environment is orderly, clean, and quiet.

7. The Servants are a part of that orderly environment. Our movements are orderly, quiet, simple.

8. Generally speaking, we may need to move much slower—in walking, in carrying, in demonstrating materials. We can move our bodies with an athlete's grace and our hands with a surgeon's skill if we put our minds to it.

We had group times at the end of the evening together. Sometimes we met in small groups. Sometimes the whole number of us were together. The following ideas referred particularly to these times together:

9. Little Seeds like to pray out loud. They like to stretch their arms up as high as they will go. They like to say Jesus' name over and over.

10. They like to lay hands on each other and pray for one another.

11. They like to make up songs. They do it all the time.

12. They like to kneel and bow low. Think of ways they can do this at a group time.

13. They like to have their questions answered in simple words.

14. They like to tell you what the group should do next. Usually they can help lead the next thing.

15. They like to be touched when they want to be touched. They don't like to be touched when they don't want to be touched.

Principle 15 was important for the Little Seeds' Servants to consider. Many adults are used to scooping children up and carrying them or tossing them or moving them about at their own whim. Or they will put their hands into a child's work and do something. Whenever this happens, the child will usually abandon the work. It is no longer his work. It has been interfered with. We seem to think that because we are bigger than they, we have special rights to do whatever we like to them at any time it strikes our fancy. This is terribly unfair. The only remedy for such thoughtless behavior is a serious consideration of the words of Jesus: "Whatever you would have others do to you, do the same to them." We would not like to be scooped up by some huge giant just as we were about to complete an intensely absorbing piece of work. We might love that giant. But the feelings that would rise up at the moment would not be loving ones. Frustration would be the mildest feeling. Children should be touched when they *should* be touched and not when we *feel* like touching them. Who is more important? We or they? We are both important. But our actions speak loudly that, with the small child, we are not always truly considerate.

The first guideline in the next list is a big help when adults come to understand it. Obedience is very important for our life with the Lord. We learn to obey. So does the child.

16. Obedience is an achievement. For the Little Seeds, they can obey only when they have sufficient control and coordination of their muscles.

17. For a Little Seed to begin, do, finish a piece of work is God's chief mode of creating order inside the Little Seed himself. We will do nothing to distract him. We usually will not so much as glance at him. And we will protect him from all interference while he works.

18. He needs encrouagement to repeat a piece of work. You can say softly, "You did it; you can do it again," as enticingly as possible.

19. The word play or toy is not used with Little Seeds. They are working. They are choosing work. They are working intently at creating.

Then there is the matter of courtesy to children. They are our brothers. We must be courteous to them. There is no reason for us to offend them. General good manners are appropriate for adults with regard to two-year-olds as well as with anyone else.

20. Little Seeds are usually twenty to forty inches tall; squat or kneel so you can look them directly in the eye. Looking at our knees is boring for them. Look at them straight so that they can see your whole face, on a level with theirs, when you are talking to them directly.

21. Talk to them quietly and distinctly. Use complete sentences. Avoid undue praise. Avoid criticism. "You finished the puzzle" is sufficient when they want you to notice that they finished a puzzle, for example.

22. If you want to speak to a child, *walk* over quietly to him. Squat or kneel and talk to him directly, so no one else needs to be involved in your conversation. He deserves this courtesy.

23. Listen to him. Smile at him and listen. Listen till he finishes what he has to say. You can always make some friendly comment like, "I'm glad you wanted to tell me that," or, "Thank you for sharing," even if you have no idea what he said.

We discussed number twenty-one at length. At last we all saw that, for the small child, verbal praise from us is a distraction. The reward for him is in the *doing* of what he did. This is altogether sufficient for him. Anything added will interfere with his concentration and his growing self-confidence.

And we saw how rude new Servants usually were, because in the beginning all felt free to call out to each other across the room or to talk over the children's heads, not considering that the room was the *children's*, whom they served, and not their own room in which to do as they pleased (see 22). The adults liked these new disciplines very much and fell into them immediately.

Greeting the children as they came each week was important. Closings and openings are very important. And at the beginning of each night the banner hanging in their view as they entered their area told them that they were in their place. We were creating spaces out of empty rooms and auditorium expanses and gymnasiums; and visual signals like banners, and boundaries like bricks and boards for shelves across an empty space, created the illusion of separation.

The banner was a big piece of maroon-colored linen, because that was the color we had. On the maroon background was glued white yarn. The white yarn formed the sketch of Jesus touching little children on the head, the sketch next to Matthew 19:14 in Good News For Modern Man (from the American Bible Society). There was the banner, week by week, hanging at the back of the Little Seeds' area and facing the gap between the partitions through which they entered. The banner's picture, Jesus patting them on the head, was their clue that they were in their right place. They were in the community of the Little Seeds. This banner was the only thing on the wall for a long time. This gave it special emphasis and importance.

And the personal greeting that each one received made the entrance very special too. They were greeted with a handshake and a smile, individually, by name, at the entering place between the partitions by one of the Servants who was set aside to do this work.

There were other "rituals" too. As soon as they came in, they quietly gathered around an overturned cardboard box. As they sat on the floor, their eyes big with watching, another Servant slowly and gracefully poured water or juice (without spilling a drop)! into ten little cups all in order. Then the Servant would carefully put the pitcher on the floor and he and another Servant would give out the cups to the children one by one. Then more would be poured till all had had his "cup of cold water in Jesus' name." The care and attention the adults gave to details were of intense interest to the small children. We had a special closed box that was filled week by week with nutritious muffins. Another Servant quietly passed among the children and offered each a muffin from the opened box while the children were drinking from the cups. The silence was deep at these times.

So they were greeted by name and then served carefully with bread and drink. It made a good beginning for the time together.

Then they drifted one by one to the materials on the shelves.

The first week after we had been asked to take responsibility for the Little Seeds, I went to the Lord in prayer about them. "Lord," I asked, "what do I do?"

"Make twenty pieces of material," came the reply in my heart.

Hmm. I got out my pencil. I got out a piece of paper. One after another I jotted down twenty things that could be done by two-year-olds. Ten clothespins in a margarine tub was one. You squeeze the clothespins open and then fasten them onto the rim of the plastic margarine tub. Then you admire what you have done, take the clothespins off one by one by squeezing them open, and put them one by one back in the margarine tub.

Then there was a nice little velvet box. Inside, I put five nuts and bolts of varying diameters. These would be screwed together and apart by some eager Little Seed.

Some small box lids! Hmm. Jo could make matching card sets to go into these. She did. Ten cards had ten different pictures of familiar household items, such as a bed, a chair, a door. Then ten more cards she made just like the first. They were scrambled together and put in one up-turned lid. Then she made ten more and their ten mates, this time with pictures of different animals. These went into the second up-turned box lid.

A shoe box with its lid on contained ten little bottles of various sizes and shapes. Each had its top on it. Each bottle opening and corresponding top was of a different diameter so that the individual bottle and top could be matched without difficulty. The bottles were for screwing on and screwing off tops.

We had used materials like this in Eric and Paula's earlier schools. I was not inventing anything new. But *twenty* different things for the Little Seeds—what else could be on the list?

Sorting, various things to sort. I acquired at a Goodwill Industries store some picnic plates with sections molded into them and a circle in the center for holding a glass. Into the center of each of the three different plates I put an assortment of buttons. One plate had buttons that felt different: leather buttons, five just alike; velvet buttons, five just alike; metal buttons, five just alike. Another plate had plastic buttons of the same design and color. But five of them were very small. Five others were twice the diameter of the little ones. And five others were in-between in size. They were mixed up together in the center circle of the plate. The third plate had buttons just alike, pretty plastic ones, but of three different shades of color—lavender, pink, and a plum color. They too were scrambled together for a sorting exercise. These were exercises to sort by feel, by size, and by color. Different points of development would be reached by the two-year-olds before they could do the different kinds of sorting.

A bowl held burrs from a gum tree, pecans, and seashells. These could be sorted into three partitions in an infant plate. A stretchable headband was laid on the bowl, in case a young one would like to try to sort the objects blindfolded. Sorting exercise number four. Let's see. What else could they do?

A fat red pincushion fit nicely on a small white tray. Five large safety pins were placed, in a row, to the right of the pincushion on the tray. They could open the safety pins, stick them carefully into the pincushion till all were in, then pull them out one by one, close them, and put them in place again on the tray.

Then I set up some pouring exercises. There was a small glass five-and-dime store tray, the kind that goes with a sugar bowl and creamer. On it I put two creamers, nose to nose, one of them half filled with colored popcorn. This was for pouring back and forth. One of our storage boxes, set up on its end, made a stand upon which sat the popcorn pouring material.

The piano bench we would cover with a big towel. Two shallow white casserole bowls fit snugly into a black plastic tray. The bowls and tray were discarded from an airline. A blue-green sponge in one of the shallow bowls completed the material. It allowed a child to stand at the side of the piano bench and squeeze water from the full bowl into the empty bowl, transferring water from bowl to bowl by means of the sponge. The smallest and most uncoordinated two-year-old could do this successfully.

On the floor was another large towel. On it I placed two small metal pans, like old-fashioned washtubs; beside these two was a larger pan. On the insides of the two small pans I taped a ring of red tape. Then I filled each small pan with water up to the top of the red taped line. I then poured both pans of water into the larger pan. At the top level of the water in the larger pan I taped another red ring. Another pouring device was ready: pouring from two smaller pans into a larger pan and then back into the smaller pans.

A little white tray, like the one on which the red pincushion sat, I put out with an eyedropper lying on it. On either side of the eyedropper was a small glass. One glass was filled two-thirds with colored water. I stored extra colored water in a jar for refills. Another "moving-water-from-one-container-to-another" material was ready. This time the child could use the eyedropper to suck up some of the colored water and then, over the empty glass, squeeze the bulb of the eyedropper and watch the colored water drip out. They liked this.

A pair of tweezers in a large jar lid was another material.

Two smaller lids fit into the large one. One little lid had five dry pinto beans in it, lying flat. The tweezers in a small hand could carefully pick up the beans one by one and transfer them to the other little lid. Back and forth, back and forth, the child could repeat the process till his heart was satisfied. No one would interrupt. No one would praise or reward. It was his own work, to do and to enjoy.

Ten empty wooden thread spools in a basket, with a black shoelace which had a washer tied to one end, made a nice stringing exercise.

On another up-turned storage box I placed a shoe-box lid turned upside down. It served to keep the work in its place as trays did for other materials. Two identical shallow plastic bowls I placed on the lid, one on each end. In one I put dry uncooked rice. I laid a spoon that had a good weight and balance to it toward the rear of the lid. The child could spoon the dry rice back and forth between the two bowls. He could put down his spoon and pick up with his fingertips any grains that he might spill in the process. It was his own work. He could do it as long as he wanted to. He only had to put it in good order when he was finished with it. As with the popcorn pouring, he could stand at the shoe-box-lid tray and work.

Two Sifo puzzles and a beautiful wood puzzle of birds that fit together into a flat wood tree came out of a teacher's cupboard. All together then we had the twenty pieces of material for the children. I had spent $1.90, most of it for little items from the Goodwill store. With the small squares of rug that someone had already given the children, we were ready to begin. They could take material from a shelf to a little rug and work with it there. The rug made the space their individual space. It told the other children and the adults, "Watch out! Don't step on this! Work in progress!"

We had no shelves those first weeks. No matter; we made the illusion of shelves. We had figured out where the materials should go on a long low board shelf, if there had been one. Then I traced each material's outline on black construction paper and cut it out. Interesting! Except for the three picnic plates which carried sorting exercises, the two Sifo puzzles, and the matching cards' boxes, everything had a different "shadow."

I took two twenty-foot stretches of wax paper and laid out upon them the "shadows." I then laid an identical stretch of wax paper on each and pressed the "shadows" between the wax paper pieces with a warm iron. The two lengths of wax paper then were our two "shelves," one each for two walls of the room. The third wall of the room we reserved for the pouring things. The fourth wall was space to pray in little groups, sing songs, and read stories.

When Sunday night came, then, we laid out one wax paper strip with its shadows inside it directly on the floor along the edge of one wall. On each shadow we carefully positioned its corresponding material. Then the second strip went down, with its material, then the storage boxes turned on end or upside down for the other materials. The piano bench received its cargo. We were ready for the Little Seeds.

Soon one of the leaders bought lengths of boards for us so that we could make proper shelves. We sanded the rough spots on the boards but we left them as boards. Each week we set them up on strong little brick-shaped cardboard boxes someone had given us. This made low shelves for the children, shelves that were about four inches off the floor. They were easy to put up beforehand, easy to take down afterwards. The strips of shadows were laid out on the boards, giving the children the exact place to return back their materials as they went back and forth to work with them each week. If the situation had been a daily one, then the children could have rapidly learned the position of everything on the shelves. But in a once-a-week situation it was better for them to have help from the shadows. They liked placing the materials exactly on their shadows. This was as pleasurable as working with the materials themselves.

For storage we used sturdy cardboard boxes that former-
ly had transported frozen chickens. There was a place for
each item in the boxes. The Servants soon learned how to
pack and unpack the boxes carefully. They were easy to
carry. And they served as "tables" upon which the uncooked popcorn pouring, the spooning, the water dripping,
and the "cup of cold water" pouring could be done.

After a while we moved into a large open area. More
boards were needed. More materials were added. Just
beyond us, but behind big folded tables, were the areas for
the four-year-olds and the five-year-olds. We wanted to
stay close to these other age groups. That way, the imma-
ture four could come around the corner into our area and do
some work that was on his level. A five-year-old could take
a two-year-old to the bathroom if the five-year-old had time
to do so. It made for some limited sharing between the children of differing sizes and abilities. We could hear each
other though. We could hear each other very well. This was
no problem during most of the evening because the busy
children were so quiet. But when each group sang toward
the end of the evening, what a noise we made! Sometimes a
grown-up with a flute might visit another group. Their
"Jesus loves me" then would drown out our "Praise Him!
Praise Him!" and we would give up and just listen.

One of the problems that we had in coping with the
physical setting of the Sunday night meetings turned into a
blessing. Problems do seem to have a way of becoming opportunities, you know. The problem was this: The parents
of the small children left them with us at a certain door.
But later that door would be locked and a teaching session
for adults would be conducted in the room behind it. That
meant that the little children had to be taken to meet their
parents at quite another location at the end of the hour and
a quarter together. Did you ever try to herd twenty or thirty

twos and threes across a gymnasium floor and get them to the same place at the same time? Impossible. Well, impossible until Earl had his brilliant idea. It was called, "*I* carry the rope."

We purchased fifty feet of heavy rope. At the end of each session with the Little Seeds, after we had prayed and done all our other group-time activities, Earl would carefully uncoil the rope and lay it stretched out flat on the floor next to the seated group. Then each child would go to the rope and take hold of it with one of his hands. We had to help the youngest ones so that they would all end up facing in the same direction: namely, the direction of the door through which we would be going. Then they would carry the rope. It was a responsibility the smallest toddler could handle: *anybody* could hold onto the rope. None of the children went too fast because they were doing the carrying and so they walked at their own speed. It took concentration. Nobody was ever tempted to let go of the rope and wander off. The process of carrying the rope was too fascinating.

And so we went, week by week, past clusters of adults, past men putting away chairs and heavy equipment, through running older children, safely, all together, carrying the rope to our destination—the Mamas and the Daddys. We were quite a sight. "Here come the Little Seeds, carrying their rope!" We could hear the admiring comments of adults as we passed. We were very important. We knew how to find our way to where we were going. And the wonderful thing about the rope was that if the destination changed, if the parents were to meet the children in another spot from the usual one, the adults ahead of the rope simply led the rope-carriers that way. We always ended up at the right place at the right time—no strays, no tears, just concentrated effort and interest.

Little things, events, and persons grow up, broaden out, to have large consequences in God's method of multiplying things.

Paula, who was eight, was in an older class during this time. She had a teacher named Sandy.

A very exciting thing happened one Sunday night. Sandy took Paula on a "faith walk." Sandy was doing this week by week with the children one by one, while her husband carried on with the rest of the group in some other activity. The "faith walk" went this way: Sandy blindfolded Paula. She took her hand. Then she led her around, inside the building and outside the building, for thirty minutes. They did not talk.

It was an exercise in feeling how we feel when God leads us. It was a special experience for Paula. It was a special experience for each child.

We lead children in ways they cannot understand. It is our responsibility to lead them in ways that keep them from harm and that take them where they need to be going— toward Jesus, toward self-assurance and acceptance. They are growing up to be all they can be in Him—happy, full of faith, and developed in all their abilities to do good work.

Be assured that small things can be the means for large change and growth for the child. I have given a detailed account of the materials which God, in the beginning of our work with the Little Seeds, led me to make. I am convinced, quite convinced, that He has specific instructions to give you in *your* situation and with *your* responsibilities. Copying what we did will not work. But imitating our going to God and asking Him to show exactly what to do and how to do it will work. It will if your heart is open to Him and if you truly want to serve the child and are willing to go to some effort to serve him. God will honor that attitude and will shower you with creativity and good sense. After all, we are on the "faith walk" ourselves. We do not understand much as we hold His hand and go with Him. But we arrive safely in the end. And you will truly arrive safely with your children if you are honestly gripping His hand.

To let God lead us is the answer. If, instead, we follow

the flow around us and fail to evaluate accepted attitudes that are contrary to God's rule and subtly counsel rebellion against Him, we will be constantly double-minded. We will be trying, impossibly, to grow Christian character, but having started with secular evaluations of human life, we will be ruled by these assumptions, not by our God. Evil influences start in little ways. But good influences do too. You can accomplish much through faithful, God-directed acts of service to your children.

Each family will have started from a different beginning in its "faith walk" with the Lord. But we will soon find ourselves doing the same things: praying, absorbing the Word, sharing, making decisions together, singing, helping one another, forgiving and encouraging one another. Through all our sensitive responses to His guidance to us, we will be yielding eagerly to His rule over us. And we shall be blessing not only Him, ourselves, and our children, but unknown persons in the future.

An Afterword

I am continually amazed, in reflecting on the goodness of our Father God, how He permits, commands, and encourages human parents to enter with Him into the creative process of shaping new young lives in righteousness and holiness to the Lord. At work together in this creative process are loving acts of our sovereign God, cherishing acts of parents who feel inadequate, and obedient responses of trusting children. How kind of the Lord to call us to participate with Him in this creation! How awesome are the responsibilities! How great are the rewards!

I encourage parents, and especially fathers, to meditate on the last verse of the Old Testament (Mal. 4:6), which speaks of the hearts of the fathers being turned to their children, and the hearts of the children to their fathers. The angel Gabriel refers to that verse in Luke 1:17. What measure of the Spirit and power of Elijah and of John the Baptist should you exercise in your children's lives, "making ready a people prepared for the Lord"?

Earl G. Alexander